Ro
Downey jr
the biography

Robert Downey Jr
the biography

Martin Howden

JOHN BLAKE

Published by John Blake Publishing Ltd,
3 Bramber Court, 2 Bramber Road,
London W14 9PB, England

www.blake.co.uk

First published in paperback in 2010

ISBN 978 1 84358 185 7

British Library Cataloguing-in-Publication Data:

A catalogue record for this book is available from the British Library.

Design by www.envydesign.co.uk

Printed in Great Britain by CPI Bookmarque Ltd, Croydon

1 3 5 7 9 10 8 6 4 2

Papers used by John Blake Publishing are natural, recyclable products made from
wood grown in sustainable forests. The manufacturing processes conform to the
environmental regulations of the country of origin.

CONTENTS

1   Childhood   1

2   Broken Homes and New Surroundings   19

3   The New Romantics   29

4   The Brat Pack Have an Opening   45

5   Robert Takes the Lead   63

6   Robert the Film Star   75

7   Comedown   87

8   Downey Goes Silent and Causes a Big Noise   101

9   Life After Chaplin   115

10   Breakdown   129

11   Robert Behind Bars   143

12   Behind Bars Once More   155

13   Robert on the Small Screen   169

14   Gibson Lends a Helping Hand   179

15   Robert Steels Himself for Future Success   223

16   Robert Steals Everyone's Thunder   237

17 Robert Gets Dramatic   245
18 Elementary My Dear Robert   253
19 Robert Still Going Strong   267
20 Robert's Future   277

1

CHILDHOOD

'I feel like I'm still looking for a home in some way'
ROBERT DOWNEY JR

The cherubic five-year-old, with his mop of hair, impish grin and big saucer eyes, fidgeted nervously on camera. Surrounded by larger-than-life adults, all waiting for him to deliver his line, he would just do his best to remember what his dad had whispered in his ear minutes earlier.

The father in question was the director and in Hollywood nothing gets you screen time faster than a parent behind the camera. Suddenly his dad shouted, 'Action!' and all the focus was on the child. With a shy but mischievous glint in his eye, Robert John Downey Jr uttered his first line on screen: 'Have you got any hair on your balls?'

As Robert explained later, 'My first acting job was

in one of my father's films called *Pound*. I played a dog. I was five. I mean, it was so strange. All the different people were playing different dogs. So the bald guy was a Mexican hairless and the guy with a silk robe on was a boxer. I played a puppy. Back then, it didn't seem that strange to me. It was just what Daddy did. And Mommy was an actress and so I went in there and I was just excited about it. I thought it was great.'

While he would go on to be acclaimed as one the greatest actors of his generation, he hadn't been cast for his acting ability. It was more a combination of his dad not having to pay for a babysitter and the lack of headache from other parents reprimanding him for getting their child to say such dialogue. Downey Sr had no such problems in letting his son off the leash, so to speak.

Even at such a young age, Robert Downey Jr believed he was working an angle to get in front of the camera. He was a natural. His easygoing acting style is no act. What some people train all their life to perfect is almost effortless to Downey. The fact that he had the acting bug was no real surprise. He was born into a family with the bohemian acting lifestyle coursing through its veins.

Downey was born in 1965 in New York to Downey Sr and Elsie Ford, arriving two years after his older sister Allyson. Downey Sr would later advise others, 'Look, whatever you do, don't name your kid after yourself. He might turn out to be more well known than you and it'll be very traumatising. We still hadn't thought up a name in the cab on the way to the hospital. It was just laziness combined with male ego.'

Underground cinema dominated Downey's childhood. Toys scattered in the living room would mingle with screening dailies on a sheet on the floor. Instead of sitting around watching TV together as a family, they would watch his father's films being put together – gathering around to see what he had shot that day.

It was a bohemian lifestyle at home, a crazy unfiltered life that created a thousand tears-of-laughter dinner-party anecdotes amid a financial environment that lurched from having no money to having lots. 'It was either toys from FAO Schwarz or, "You guys mind mayonnaise sandwiches again?"' remembered Robert.

'My father always said that money isn't important. It was definitely feast or famine, that's for sure. One thing I've learned, when there's money, you really make up for times when there isn't.'

Other early childhood memories include his dad attempting to read the mind of their Yorkshire terrier Sturgess and mixing his drinks with an upside-down hammer. Robert remembers his mother coming to pick him up at school, wearing a 'quilted cape' and the time he struggled against the pull of the sea while holding onto his dad's feet in the water – with Downey Sr blissfully unaware of his son's plight. 'He was six foot three and I was probably three-and-a-half or four. It seemed to me that he wasn't even aware that every time the waves came in and went out, he was saving my life. And all I had to do was hold on hard enough, just hard enough to have the pull of the wave dissipate.'

Robert also remembers being on his dad's shoulders as he walked through Greenwich Village and an early Christmas memory of his dad in a Superman shirt, surrounded by presents. They would only tell him that they were from Santa.

'I had to figure this out,' he remembered. 'This is probably a good metaphor for the general haphazardness of doing what we did. My father once ordered gravel to widen our driveway, but the guys in the truck brought the wrong size, rocks bigger than your fist. And Dad didn't care. He was like, "Ah, just put 'em down." So driving up the driveway, you'd risk piercing the gas tank. I think about this now and it drives me nuts. The idea of: a) some guy taking us for a ride, pulling a joke on this city hippie; and b) my father just allowing it, saying yeah, making a long-term decision off the top of his head. And I've done the same thing.'

The family insisted on open communication, with no subject too taboo to broach. 'I had my dad hanging out with the coolest, smartest, maverick fucking weirdos of the twentieth century in New York,' Robert recalled fondly. 'I used to fall asleep listening to my dad's poker games – and they were only playing poker so that they could riff on lines and put-downs. So I heard this rhythm: it'd be quiet and then someone would hit it and they'd all fucking lose it. It was like winning the pot wasn't about the chips.

'That, to me, used to be the most comforting feeling going to sleep at night, just hearing that. This is what men are supposed to do – this two-layered thing – and it's about wit and repartee and a lot of sarcasm.'

His father was an eccentric among eccentrics – a darling of the art house film world. 'He was a real auteur, maverick guy,' is how Downey would describe him. 'He was the original and I would not be doing this if it was not for him.

'[They were] artistic and revered East Coast squares who happened to like marijuana,' he added. 'Even the counter-cultural guys couldn't relate to them. When Dad got into coke, he didn't really know how dangerous it was. He was very naive. He just thought it helped him edit. To me, we were an artistic family trying to find normalcy. Marijuana was a staple – like rice!'

Robert's father was born Robert Elias, but ended up taking his stepfather's surname (James Downey) in his youth. In fact, he had wanted to call himself just Elias: 'I thought that it would be such a shocking, significant and incendiary rearrangement that it would also rearrange my fragmented psyche.'

Downey Sr was a restless soul, always searching for

an outlet. By the time he reached his early twenties, these outlets would include time served in the army, becoming a boxing champion, an amateur baseball player and writing for the stage. He had enlisted in the army at the age of 16, faking a birth certificate using his father's name to show he was the legal age. If that showed inventiveness and a degree of passion on Downey Sr's part, that enthusiasm soon began to fade.

Downey Sr recalled, 'I had a fight with the lieutenant. I used to drink then. I drank, got into a fight with the officer. Ended up in the stockade. I went to a dance in town in my civvies. About an hour after I'd left, the sergeant came up and yelled, "Downey, need any chow?" And I wasn't there. And then he drove to the dance and walked in and saw me there. I got three months for that.'

Reading somewhere that anybody could make a movie, he decided he would put the theory into practice while in detention. 'I started writing stuff down, writing scenes, trying to write a novel. I was happy with it.' Out of the army at 19, he 'found a cameraman and shot some stuff. It was trial and error and usually more error, but it was exciting.'

Luckily, the nearby Charles Theatre in New York would show new kinds of films. 'Anybody could bring a film. You just had to have it there three hours before they showed it. Some very interesting filmmakers came out there. It was an exciting time to make a movie and express yourself, without having to go to meetings.'

The low-budget 16mm short *Balls Bluff* marked Downey Sr's debut in 1961. It would be followed over a seven-year period by *A Touch of Greatness*, *Babo 73*, *Sweet Smell of Sex*, *Chafed Elbows* and *No More Excuses*.

Downey Sr proposed to actress Elsie Ford on their third date at a baseball game, and in 1963 the couple welcomed their daughter, Allyson. Downey Sr and Elsie would work together on 1966's *Chafed Elbows* – a film that saw her play all the female roles despite being pregnant with Robert.

Downey Sr's work divides opinions, with critics dismissing it as unsubtle satire minus the laughs, while his fans revel in the single-minded madness. What is unarguable is that his early films are his vision and his alone. They would be full of guerilla filming tactics that would cement his name as one of the influential new-wave directors who hit US cinemas in the late 1960s and early 1970s.

The *New York Times* wrote, 'One of these days, Robert Downey is going to clean himself up a good bit, wash the dirty words out of his mouth and do something worth mature attention in the way of kooky, satiric comedy. He has the audacity for it. He also has the wit.'

In the 1964 war satire *Babo 73*, Downey Sr went to the White House and secretly filmed his lead actor, Taylor Mead, posing as the President of the United

States. 'Because [President] Kennedy wasn't there, there wasn't that tough a security. I'm running down with a wind-up camera that gets you twenty-two seconds before you have to wind it again. Of course, the generals would come past and he'd salute them like the President and they would look all confused, which would suit the film perfectly.'

While many critics dismissed the movie (*Village Voice* called it 'infantile' and 'shambling'), one called it the funniest film of the year, enabling the director to secure funding for more movies, one of which would be 1969's *Putney Swope*.

The satirical film, which many feel is Downey Sr's best work, tells the story of an African-American man accidentally being put in charge of a prestigious advertising firm. Deciding to 'not rock the boat but sink it', Swope renames the agency Truth and Soul, Inc – and havoc inevitably ensues.

The germ of the idea came after Downey Sr worked at the experimental division of an ad agency. '[There was] a white guy – me – and a black guy who said, "Bob, me and you are doing the same job but you're making more money." I said, "Let's go talk to the boss about it." And we went in and he stated his case. And the boss said, "If I give you more money, I've got to give Bob more money and we're right back where we started from." I thought, "God, that's worth a movie."'

Putney Swope would go on to become a success at

the box office, where it came out two weeks after *Easy Rider* – another counter-culture favourite. 'When *Putney Swope* came out,' Robert remembered, 'Dad thought it would be wise for us all to leave the country. So me, my mom and my sister moved with him to London. I was five. Dad said he chose London because after what was going on in New York, he wanted to go somewhere really boring.'

London was something of a culture shock to young Robert. 'I spent half my school days there in a corner because the teachers would say, "Robert," and I'd say, "What?" then they'd say, "Don't say 'What', say 'Excuse me',", and I'd say, "Huh?" and they'd say, "Go and stand in the corner." However brief, I didn't enjoy England's educational system. The teachers seemed awfully uptight.' In another interview he said, 'I spent my whole time there with my nose in the corner, being a moron.'

Following the success of *Putney Swope*, there were brief meetings with Hollywood bosses for Downey Sr, but he was reluctant to give up his creative freedom. Next up was 1970's *Pound*, which saw the family move back to New York for Robert's aforementioned screen debut. Sadly it failed to replicate the success of *Putney Swope*. It didn't help that United Artists were somewhat surprised when Downey Sr handed in his edit. 'They thought it was going to be animated. They didn't think it was going to be live action. It threw them. It wasn't fun. It ended up as a double bill and it would be X-rated for language, not violence.'

Frustrated by the studio's meddling, Downey Sr managed to secure independent funding for his next movie *Greaser's Palace* easily enough. 'This lady wanted me to make a movie. She gave the script to her husband, who had a lot of money. And he said to me, "Is this going to make any money?" I said, "I don't think so." He said to his wife, "He's charming – give him the money."'

Greaser's Palace would feature another appearance by young Robert, in which, rather unnervingly, he would have his throat slit by God. He wasn't the only family member to suffer. 'My mom really got it from God,' Robert said. 'She got arrows, she got shot.'

'It could have been too much to expose him to,' Downey Sr would later admit. 'It was traumatic for him to see that kind of violence. He didn't comprehend that everybody comes back again.'

However, after working with his mother, this was the film that really sowed the seeds of becoming an actor in his mind. 'That was when I recognised that there was someone in my family who worked in front of the camera and her work had a deep effect on people who were watching. That was also when I realised it was a discipline you had to do again and again. I didn't want to do it again.'

His father remembered, 'We were doing a scene with this big crew in New Mexico. We did a first take... I told him that he's done a terrific job and he wanted to go back to the house. I said, "No, I need another take." He said, "Why? I got it right – why do I have to do it again?"

'The crew started laughing at me, he shook his finger at me and said, "One more time, that's it." We did it again, but a bird flew through the frame. And he refused to do it again!' But Downey Sr insisted. It was a lesson his son says he's never forgotten.

Because of his boyish enthusiasm, Robert was the centre of attention on set. 'I was a little… undersized. I don't know if I was looking for approval so much as looking for a connection. But it's a strange place to feel connected – with a bunch of relative strangers, doing something false.'

But in a household packed with larger-than-life characters – whether family members or the eccentric actors who would gather at Downey's house – acting ensured attention, which suited Robert perfectly. He was cheeky, cocksure and dramatic, all aided by a flamboyant flourish – traits that would see him through most of his adult life, as well as his childhood years.

'I was seven or eight, in the first grade,' he recalled, 'and we were doing this play in the classroom. I stood in the hallway, then I made my entrance into the classroom and I think I said, "Yield the castle now, Lady Roxanne." And people liked the fact that I had the confidence to say that. It just worked. I felt confident.'

'That's all he ever wanted to do,' Downey Sr said.

'When we put him in *Pound* he resisted, but by the time he left you could see that's exactly what he wanted. He was very good from the beginning.'

Robert added, 'The eternal child thing I get from my dad. But the love of being a performer, I definitely get that from my mom. [Allyson] was the smart one, going to private school, and I was the one who made the company laugh at dinner. I worked at it – I wanted to be entertaining.'

School was less of a place of education for Robert than one he hoped would be a shelter of normality, for his family were constantly on the move. 'Junior was born in Manhattan,' Downey Sr has said. 'Then we moved to Forest Hills. Then a loft in Greenwich Village. London. New York again. New Mexico. Los Angeles. Connecticut. Woodstock. New York. Los Angeles again. Back to New York. Back to Los Angeles. It was crazy.'

Robert has said, 'I thought that in some ways my dad was an absent father, but he'd be there for every Christmas. He'd go out of town a lot, but he was pretty much there a lot more than most dads. Now that I do have to leave town sometimes and go to places, I go, "Wow, it's really hard to be there all the time for your kid no matter what." I guess what's important is the quality of the time when you are with them.'

Many media commentators have speculated that his adult life has been that of a nomad striving for domesticity. However, for a large part of his life that aspect of his childhood was pushed into the background in favour of a much darker one – and one that later threatened to define him, rather than his natural talents.

He was eight when he first sampled drugs. It was at one of his parents' house parties, where the inquisitive young Robert spotted a marijuana joint lying around and promptly decided to smoke it.

Downey Sr reasoned later, 'I think that a lot of us did things and thought it would be hypocritical to not have our kids participate in marijuana and stuff like that. So we thought it was cute to let them smoke it. And all that was an idiot move on our parts to share that with our children.'

Downey Sr recalled one such occasion to *Vanity Fair*: 'We were all sitting around, smoking grass and playing poker down the old West Village loft and Robert was staring at me kind of funny. Robert was always an observer of it all, even at a very young age. And I go, "You know, you ought to try a little of this instead of drinking." I passed him a joint. And suddenly I knew I had made a terrible, stupid mistake. Giving a little kid a toke of grass just to be funny. The story keeps getting repeated. I'll never forgive myself, but Robert and I have dealt with it and he's said to me, "I'm not a victim, Dad, I don't blame anybody."'

'To put our growing up into the context of right now,' said Allyson, who is far more critical of her family than Robert, 'it would be the equivalent of having Quentin Tarantino as your father. My family were all great characters. I don't know, though, that they were great family members. We're all good characters, we all definitely occupy that spot.'

One of Allyson's friends said about her childhood, 'We never really spoke about it, because they [Robert and Allyson] kept it hush-hush.' According to the friend, whenever Allyson's childhood was brought up, she would say, 'Let it be.' She certainly had her own battles with personal demons, including drug addiction and an eating disorder. She would add that her and Robert's childhood was lacking in adult guidance and that it was something of a 'nightmare'.

'But because Robert's never known what it means to be happy, it's not such a sore spot with him. He has no frame of reference. He's done the best that he can and recognises that something is missing, but he can't necessarily put his finger on it. The world Robert lives in, his emotional reality, it's so overwhelming for him just to function. He's like an idiot savant. He's a brilliant actor, a brilliant person and a really good friend. But he has handicaps in dealing with day-to-day situations.

'I think that it's also the pain that he is in. And it's been with him for a long time. Like me, I don't think he uses drugs so much to feel anything as to not feel anything, to block out all the emotions – just so he can function.'

Robert would later say, 'Though I feel resentment

sometimes, I don't think I have any more reason to resent than someone in the sixteenth century who was leeched by his dad. I mean, it really was the times. I was in the generation that was smoking pot. I lived in Woodstock, where it was like rainbows and pinball and pizza and pot.'

Downey Sr commented in an interview years later, 'We thought, "Why be a hypocrite?" We should have been hypocrites. I was a real jerk about drugs. I've felt tremendous guilt. It's only now finally leaving me.'

In another interview, Robert added, 'I liked being my dad's kid. I liked the respect he got. I loved his sense of humour. I loved watching my mom make movies. And that's when I really got into it. When my mom kind of retired, I started and I felt in a way that I carried that on. I think if I'd come from a conservative family, I'd probably be swinging from a rope. In my dad's work, underneath the comedy there was always something poignant. Comedy isn't comedy without something behind it. It's just entertainment without that additional layer.'

It shouldn't be any surprise that Robert would go on to be an actor. While the camera's prying eye would be a dominant factor growing up – 'My sister would look at me funny, I'd turn around to smack her and there'd be a 16mm camera filming it all. To me, it just kind of seemed like a day-to-day thing' – it was also the one thing that Robert sensed would get his father's attention. With his sister being the smarter one of the two, according to Robert, he would rely on his wit and his need to perform.

'Mom and Dad's generation – being available to your kids wasn't necessarily as important as getting out there and being an independent filmmaker or an independent woman,' Robert has said.

There is a telling moment in a 1991 interview with Downey Sr. When asked how old his son was during the making of *Pound*, he was flustered. 'It was 1970, so...' There was a ten-second pause, before he said, 'Five,' followed by a somewhat sheepish laugh.

Robert would later joke about telling his dad he wanted to be an actor, saying, 'I think he was indifferent. My dad says anybody can act and few can direct and nobody can write. On a scale of one to ten, being an actor was about the least honourable of those three.'

But at ten years old, what Robert cared about was making sure that everyone knew he was around. 'He was a real character,' said Richard Allen, who attended Stagedoor Manor summer camp (in the Catskill Mountains of New York state) with Robert. 'Walking around in sunglasses with a cockiness most kids his age – or any age – rarely possess. He and Allyson were very mature, much cooler than most of the mainly suburban kids who populated the camp.'

Robert and his 13-year-old sister attended the prestigious performing arts summer camp in 1975 – and the pair of them certainly left an impression on their fellow campers. 'They were both more cynical and worldly than the average kid,' remembered Allen, who would later remark about Downey Sr and Elsie, 'I don't think they were great parent material.'

While Allyson would be aloof and sometimes distant, yet brimming with intelligence when asked questions, camp counsellor Todd Graff remembered that Robert would be 'insanely hyperactive' and a 'pain in the ass'.

Robert attended the camp for three years running, putting on plays and choreographing dance moves. He wasn't the most popular kid there – some people thought he acted the big shot because of his dad, while others were intrigued by the confidence he projected, forced or not – but he was certainly one of the most notable.

It may not have been a normal childhood for Robert, but it certainly was an interesting one. Then, as he entered his teens, the world came crashing down on him.

2

BROKEN HOMES AND NEW SURROUNDINGS

*'If my father were less of a pioneer, he
probably would have been more of a father,
but I wouldn't be who I was'*
ROBERT DOWNEY JR

'I grew up in a family that was doing drugs and trying to be creative. At the same time there was so much love and laughter in our family,' was how Robert described his childhood. 'But at fourteen my mom and dad's marriage was over.'

'In the 1970s, I was such a mess,' Downey Sr recalled. 'It was a disaster. Coke is such a waste of time. A total waste of time.'

The break-up, according to Robert, devastated his mother. 'They were married and had been creative partners for fifteen years,' he said. 'They were partners more than husband and wife: there was a great sense of humour and irony in their relationship and the separation left her shell-shocked. My sister went to live with my dad. [She] was the one they had sent to private school and thought was going to do great things. I was this weird pothead kid who got off blowing away things with my BB gun. I went with my mom because she needed me.'

First Robert and his mother lived 'in this little apartment that wasn't comfortable for either of us'.

'We moved to 19 E 48th Street, between Madison and Fifth. It was a five-floor walk-up to this depressing fucking place with no windows. Well, there were windows but there were bars on them and there was always this grainy, gray light coming through them. It always seemed like it was six pm. I can't relate to real poverty, but we were cooking on a burner instead of an oven and we were trying to create this sense of family or happiness in the skankiest of surroundings.'

While he was there for his mother, his early teenage years saw Robert 'rifling through my mother's purse for money' on a regular basis. 'I probably confiscated a good twenty to sixty per cent of her alimony first thing in the morning before I went to school,' he joked later. He would hang out in Washington Square with his friends, get into scrapes with kids from a local club and regularly watch the stage production of *The Rocky Horror Picture Show*.

'For a teenager, it was rather confusing,' Robert recalled of his lifestyle. 'Always on the move, hanging out with this group here and that group there... due to the drugs I was taking... I was completely inaccessible. I was not dealing with life in an effective manner. Instead, I was creating a separate reality from the one in which I now live and was dealing with that reality the best I could.'

Realising that 'living with your mom in an apartment, you couldn't even have a girlfriend', and desperate to be part of a 'teenage scene', he moved to California to live with his dad. It was quite a change. 'You go from the one-room apartment on 48th Street to the house with the pool,' Robert recalled.

Rather than finding the move a huge culture shock, Robert used his new surroundings to forge a new identity for himself as he attended first Lincoln Junior High School and then Santa Monica High School. His classmates at first thought he was a tough guy because of his New York background – and he duly obliged. Striving to fit in, he would play up to the image by cycling around Santa Monica with a knife tucked under his socks.

He would go on to hang out with the Estevez clan. With Martin Sheen as a father and Charlie Sheen and Emilio Estevez as siblings, the Estevez clan was something of an acting dynasty. Robert, however, hung out mostly with the middle son, Ramon. '[Ramon] taught me how to tap-dance,' said Robert. 'He taught me about the social intricacies of late-night coffee shops. He was the first true eccentric I ever met.

21

They lived in Malibu. They all drove nice cars. They had a tight family.'

Santa Monica High School was the place that sealed Robert's love for acting –his primary reason for attending. One of the school productions was the musical *Oklahoma!* which saw him showcase the tap-dancing skills he had learned from Ramon. '[He] would come by and pick me up in this oversized red Cadillac convertible,' Robert remembered. "Can you imagine me, the weirdo from New York, and him, the punk rocker with blue hair, tap-dancing in a studio in front of a mirror?'

Robert's classmates have different memories of him. To some, he was a bright and zany kid – a school jester who was 'outspoken, had a lot of confidence and was popular'. To others, he was 'arrogant and pretentious', according to one pupil. 'Not the brightest bulb, but the cockiest of them all. He had no qualms of saying he was going to be a movie star – his dad told him so. I'll give him credit for accomplishing a path he had set when he was only thirteen or so.'

Certainly, Robert's adult persona – cocksure arrogance, blunted by a playful charm and a smattering of self-deprecation – hadn't quite been honed yet. 'Robert used to rub it in everybody's faces his dad was a producer and director,' recalled stage-door camper Dina McLelland. 'He wasn't a nice kid. He had an attitude of being better than everybody else because of who his dad was.

'I didn't know who his dad was. I do now. But someone kept saying, "Oh, he thinks he's all hot shit because his dad's a producer/director type." And I was like, "Have I seen any [of his movies]?"'

In fact, Robert did appear in his dad's 1980 film *Up the Academy* – although the minor role would be uncredited.

But there was no doubt Robert was something of a talent in drama, saying, in typical blunt style, 'At Santa Monica High I read *The Twelve Rules of Theatre* and that's easy stuff, but I think I did learn, because we did *Oklahoma!* and *Detective Story*. We did *The Rivals* by Richard Sheridan and I played Captain Absolute. I learned how to tap-dance and sing. I was being trained to be in a bunch of revivals in regional theatres.'

Winning the Biggest Flirt award at drama school, Robert was also something of a lady magnet. Dubbed 'Studley Moore' by his friends, he embarked on a series of dates with some of the most popular and beautiful girls at his school.

His school friend Chris Bell told Ben Falk, author of the book *The Fall and Rise of the Comeback Kid*, 'We used to go to the Santa Monica Place [shopping centre], which was brand new at the time. He proceeded to get up and walk through the fountain inside the mall, which was a large round pool with a jet of water shooting up in the centre. He walked right through it. We were kind of amused and horrified at the same time and he was immediately hauled away by the mall security. We had to wait about twenty-five minutes for him to be released and told not to come back into the mall again. That story encapsulates a lot of qualities in being his friend – fun, very extravagant and wild. But you also have to pick up the pieces that come with it. There's a problematic side to that. There were definitely some over-the-top moments.'

Despite his love for the school acting programme, Robert was becoming disillusioned with life at Santa Monica High. 'I would show up in the morning and hang out with my friends, then ditch,' he said. 'Show up for theatre arts, ditch. Come back to hook up after school. There was this fence – that's where I learned to escape. It wasn't easy to get over this chain-link fence, which was twenty feet high, at least.'

Bell would say of Robert when he first met him, 'I consider my time with him to be much more innocent. Before the drugs, before things got too jaded and dating was very new. I was never one to party too much in terms of drugs but I knew he was starting to hang out with people who were a little more on the dark side. That was never appealing to me. It's amazing when I look back at all the drugs that were in high school, at our disposal.'

However, it wasn't all innocence. 'We were at a party of a friend of ours in Santa Monica,' Bell recalled, 'and I had my mom's car, this old Mercedes. We had been drinking and I remember a few of us went to go and sit down for some reason to get away from the party, to chat. We sat in my mom's car. He was looking quite out of it and he goes, "I just want to sit here for a little bit," so I left him there. Suddenly, we're in this party and someone said, "I just saw Robert two blocks down the street being arrested!" And we were like, "What?" He'd driven off in my mom's car! I got the car back and I remember his dad was very upset. A group of us had to go down to Santa Monica Police Station and that's where I got my mom's car keys back.'

Robert would end up with his first DUI charge, though his relationship at the time with his dad remained a good one. He always had a lot of freedom and did what teenage boys do, sitting inside eating a lot of junk food and watching countless horror films.

'My generation was so independent,' he recalled. 'I remember telling my dad, "I'm going to go and see Allyson at her school in Vermont." He'd say, "Oh yeah, what's that going to run me?" "Seventy-five dollars round trip and twenty-five dollars for me." "OK." I walked out of the door. I was thirteen. It was great, but on the other hand... I think my parents thought this hands-off thing really seemed to work.'

Allyson would add, 'I went away one summer and by the time I came back, Robert had converted my room into a love nest, a bachelor room. He didn't tell his friends I was back; they'd come in, in the middle of the night and try to make out on top of me!'

Robert finally left school at 17. 'I quit school in eleventh grade. I said to my dad, "Can I tell my counsellor that I'm quitting?" He said, "Either show up every day or quit, whatever you want. Do something productive." I said, "Oh, thanks, Dad." So I went to school and my theatre-arts teacher said, 'Are you going to be around for *Romeo and Juliet*?' And I said, "Well, I don't think so. I think I'm going to clear out my locker right now and quit school."

'So I went into my counsellor's office and she was like, "Oh, Robert, if you stay through the summer, you can make up these six hundred credits and you can spend your whole summer under fluorescent lighting and then, well, you might be able to get into your last year of high school."

'And I said, "I think I'll just quit instead." She's like, "Oh, we'll call your father about that." She called my dad and he's like, "Sure, whatever he wants to do, as long as he gets a job and is productive." And I said, "I told you so," and walked out of school.'

So at 17, Robert had decided that his future would lie in being an actor. He was certainly bullish about his talents. 'There's no one that can act better than me. There's no one that will go places that I will go,' he used to say, although years later he admitted that such comments were nothing more than 'an egomaniac with an inferiority complex'.

Looking back on childhood experiences that had included taking drugs at an early age, travelling across the world, his parents separating, living with his mother then his father, run-ins with the law and a desperate yearning to fit in, Robert said, 'It just accelerated my learning that much more. If my father were less of a pioneer, he probably would have been more of a father, but I wouldn't be who I was.

'I'm not a bitter ball about it. We can all choose our experiences on some level. There are no victims. If I hear one more person say they're destroyed because they never got their dad's approval... That's self-centred to the extreme. I'm tired of the faux depression thing. It's an excuse to take your favourite medications.'

It had certainly been quite a childhood, but it was only the start of Robert's fascinating and incident-packed life. He was now leaving school and heading back to where it had all begun for him – New York and the film environment that was something of a comfort blanket to him.

It's easy to theorise why Robert would want to make a career of the very same activity that his family, whose approval he desperately wanted, did. While it was clear that it was something he was pretty good at, it should be remembered that Robert has never seen making movies as an art form. Yes, he wanted to show people he had a talent but by and large he wasn't set on making the greatest film of all time. The films he liked were popcorn movies, fun, disposable pieces of entertainment that were meant to do just that – to entertain.

When he was finally able to make those kinds of films decades later, there would be accusations of selling out from certain sections – but it was never his intention to be an actor specialising in art-house pictures. No, he wanted to be a movie star. He may not have walked the walk of a typical leading man and he has never played the studio game, but he was desperate to be in a movie and by God he would make sure he was the best thing in any film he would be in.

'My initial goals were external. I wanted to make a million dollars. I wanted my name above the titles and I wanted everyone to know who I was and all my friends going, "Wow, I wish I were him." It probably wouldn't have made me any happier but at least it would have given me the guise of success.'

And so he headed back to New York with grand dreams of making it. But just like his childhood, it was to be a journey packed with drama.

3

THE NEW
ROMANTICS

'I believed I was the person holding him together'
SARAH JESSICA PARKER

O nce back in New York, Robert attempted to eke
out a living while trying to become an actor. He
sold shoes, waited on tables and performed in a 'living
art' exhibition at the Area nightclub. 'I worked in one
of those glasses cases. I was wearing an orange space
suit, sending Gumby dolls... in plastic bubbles...
down a conveyor belt. It was great – all the young
actors would come in. I was a sideshow for their
weekend. But I didn't really care. I had fun playing to
the fourth wall all night... for $10 an hour and all the
brandy I could muster.'

He lived with his sister for a spell and also found
himself a small apartment on 9th Avenue and 52nd
Street in midtown Manhattan. 'There were no windows

that you could see out of. I just remember it being a really depressing, claustrophobic space that I actually had a lot of fun in. I was a busboy at Central Falls restaurant. I don't think it was tough monetarily. As a matter of fact it was the best thing that ever happened to me when my dad said, "I've carried you for too long. You're eighteen. Don't call me up to even ask me for a dollar. I don't care if you tell me you're hungry." I remember that was the point of transition where I decided, "Fuck, I really have to grow up now..." That's part of education, the moment when your dad says, "The gravy train is done." I was living with my sister in a really depressing apartment on Edgar Allan Poe Street, West 84th Street. Really depressing. I'd put on whatever clothes I had and I would go on these casting calls. I didn't have an agent.'

It was a chance for Robert to gain independence, a chance for him to do something for himself and a chance to show that he had the talent and drive to become an actor. In fact, according to Robert, his mother said the last time 'she saw me with any real humility was when I was seventeen, doing theatre in New York'.

'You know, truthfully, I've never seen Bobby happy – really, really happy,' she would say in 2000. 'But I haven't seen many people happy. I've never seen him enjoy life – he enjoys lives. You only know so much about how to raise children. I always wanted him to be happy.'

Robert loved spending time with his sister and the feeling was mutual. Fiercely protective of Robert, Allyson would do everything she could to make him happy. Although one occasion – burned into her memory – stretched her patience to breaking point. She received a phone call from him while out in New York. 'He called me, all pathetic, "Ally, I have pneumonia, bring me orange juice." I get to his place and there's about thirty girls rubbing his feet, feeding him through an eye dropper.'

As in his school years, Robert had found attracting girls pretty easy. 'There was a time I could meet practically any woman, if her defences were down, and have her throw down her purse to hold me. It's the "vulnerable" thing,' he said.

But Robert quickly discovered how tough it would be to forge an acting career. He might have a famous dad – especially in New York acting circles – but he discovered it didn't mean anything. My dad didn't mind if I came out here, but he wasn't going to really help me. My dad stood up at the Directors Guild and told them all to go fuck themselves, so it wasn't like he was helping me get jobs. He said, "Don't use my name and don't be too obnoxious in interviews."

'But it was weird. I'd go in to an interview and they'd say, "Hi, Robert, let's talk about your dad." And then an hour and a half later we'd be laughing, having a great time and they'd say, "See ya." I'd be out the door and we never even talked about the role... It didn't hamper or help me, really. No one knew who he was when I'd go to meetings. Or people who did would just say, "That's nice. Let's see if we like *you* or not."

'I didn't get trained in drama school; it was all on the job. That shit costs money; my dad was an underground filmmaker. I was faking it, to try to fit in with the kids who really were Professional Children's School or Performing Arts. If you look at what was going on in 1983 in Manhattan for kids, by the time you were fourteen you'd wept to *Jacques Brel is Alive and Well and Living in Paris*; you'd done a Jules Feiffer one-act; you'd seen *West Side Story* done as well as it would ever be. We all went up for everything from Casio commercials to *Once Upon a Time in America*. We were kind of learning how to be in music videos, all dancing about and singing.

'I did the entire Sanford Meisner process just by hanging around and smoking weed in the stairways with my friends who had just gotten back from class. They'd tell me the exercises. It seemed like inevitably they would end up screaming and crying – screaming at each other and crying at what was screamed. I would just call that Thanksgiving.'

But while he was finding it tough, he didn't do himself any favours, as Allyson remembered. 'He put in a couple of years in New York offending everybody to get known. He'd go to an audition for an all-black film, for example, and convince everyone in the waiting room that he had the part. So they'd leave. And there were no roles for whites in the movie.'

At another audition he was flippant and aloof, answering a TV director's question 'How do you support yourself when you're not working as an actor?' with the line, 'My spine.' Not surprisingly, he didn't land the role.

It was a mixture of self-belief bordering on reckless arrogance, and he would carry that forward to his opinions on acting teachers. 'I'm a real prick about acting coaches. I have nothing to learn from somebody who's never made it as an actor himself. Then I wind up feeling bad for the guy. Maybe he's a fucking drunk and he's saying, "It's like this." No, it's not like that. Fuck it, man.'

Robert had no real idea about how to begin a career as an actor within the studio system. As he readily admits, he had no idea 'what a fuckin' pilot season was' – a potentially lucrative time for actors when the major TV producers record an episode of a promising new show in a bid to get commissioned for a series.

For Robert, based on his father's experience, making a movie was part of the hustle – trying to grab financial support on the fly and thinking on your feet. The studios, however, were far more organised than that – and didn't seem to care much for a livewire son of a maverick director.

Eventually, however, Robert would land parts on

the stage, including productions of *American Passion* and the gay drama *Fraternity*. 'It wasn't so much that I decided to become an actor as it was that acting was something good for me to do, something I wanted to do. Most of the things in my life were pursued out of necessity, not out of desire. I had this extreme paranoia that led me to be good. I was so afraid of not having my shit together. I'd get to the theatre an hour and a half before every show, stretch out on this mat and run over actions and transitions in my head. This paranoia gave me discipline. The other guys would come in and say, "Downey's gone to Nirvana again."

'What's weird is that, at that time in my life, I was also just getting into spiritual stuff – like the human energy systems, auras and projections of consciousness. I felt like it wasn't even me going out to get all of these books – it was my higher self saying, "Fuck, this kid's in trouble; we better surround him with a lot of good thoughts."

Learning was proving to be a slow process, but one he was determined to persevere with. Stage fright, he said, was 'like a pleasant pain in your stomach, because you know you're about to do something you want to do, especially if your parents are there, or your peers. Your parents are going to be supportive... which is great. Your really good friends will just say, "It was weak," or "It was good..." Sometimes you learn the most from your worst experiences.'

Robert stuck at it, continuing to work as a busboy while feeding off scraps of minor roles on the stage. He would eventually land an agent and soon afterwards he was in front of the camera for his screen debut proper. The film was *Baby It's You* – a romantic drama by American maverick director John Sayles.

It felt like a huge vindication for Robert, but his joy was to be short lived. After working on the film for four weeks, he discovered that the final cut saw him relegated to a minor role. As he said to *Rolling Stone* in 1988, 'I told all my friends I was now, officially, a major talent and film star. And then they cut my scenes out. You don't even see me except in one scene – you see me in the background until this self-indulgent actress leans forward to try and get more camera time.' His friends would soon dub the film *Maybe It's You*.

It was certainly a chastening experience for Robert, who had left LA with high hopes – ambitions that typically he wasn't shy about telling people. Chris Bell, his friend while growing up in LA, remembers Robert telling him that he had a lot of industry contacts. 'He was promised this big career. We were all very happy for him.'

The film's producer Amy Robinson was convinced, though, that Robert would be back on the big screen. 'Really talented people never really go away,' she said later. 'They wax and they wane. The movie was the first part he had other than in one of his father's movies – it was a big step forward. Maybe.'

Robert was to get better luck in his next role in *Firstborn* – a drama by British director Michael Apted, which would also star Corey Haim and Sarah Jessica Parker. He was only in a handful of scenes, but his frantic mannerisms and manic, rapid-fire delivery were evident even then – and fully showcased his potential as an actor who could dominate a scene with even a fleeting appearance.

It was the first real example of undiluted Downey on screen, but the film would have another lasting impact on his life, because of his relationship with one of his co-stars. Robert would have dalliances with actresses in latter years, admitting, 'I remember certain colleagues having a lot of fun on the set with me. Every second star goes to bed with his co-star because they spend so much time together. But I'm not going to start reeling off the names.'

It was different with Parker, however. Theirs was a passionate and meaningful relationship that saw both jump in the deep end straight away. Robert moved into her apartment two weeks after they met. 'We fell in love big time,' he said.

'I dated a lot of girls, but most of them were interested in me because they thought I was going somewhere, not because of who I really was. [Sarah] was sitting across the room and I thought, "You have a lot to learn from this person." I guess Sarah thought

I looked scary enough to be interesting,' he said. Small wonder, really – with his spiky punk hair and glasses with Superman stickers on them.

They would take the cab to the set of *Firstborn* but always get out before they reached the set so no one would notice. 'The relationship was so impetuous, we were almost embarrassed for anyone to know,' Parker said. 'What I really remember about Downey is how smart and funny and fast and relentless he was. I'd never encountered that kind of humour before and I was mad for it. He's not your run-of-the-mill funnyman. So much of his work is improv. It's literally flying out of his mouth. There's no one else like him.'

The two actors would have fun together – jogging in Central Park or having water balloon fights with their neighbours. 'You have to run to each window and hope you get there in time to close it,' she said in an interview. 'It's very immature, I know, but fun.'

While he gave her confidence being around people, she offered him stability in return – opening a bank account for him, for example. It's no surprise that Robert would dub her 'the best thing that ever happened to me'.

Downey Sr said about their relationship, 'I thank God for Sarah Jessica Parker. Without her, Robert would go at a hundred miles per hour into a brick wall. They're very sweet together. He might become a gentleman as a result of this.'

Parker's mother was less than excited about the

pair's relationship, however. She was unsure about the speed with which her daughter was rushing into a relationship with Robert. In fact, the actress did her best to put off telling her mother about her new boyfriend.

It was clear, though, the pair were becoming incredibly close. There was definitely a Yin and Yang aspect to their relationship and they shared the emotional difficulties of coming from a home with parental difficulties.

Parker had been raised in Ohio by her mother and stepfather, in a household that had some financial hardships, including times when the electricity was cut off. She was desperate to make a name for herself in showbiz – be it in music or acting. She was certainly an accomplished dancer, earning a scholarship in a Cincinnati music college. To help achieve her dreams, her family moved to New York, where she landed several gigs in adverts and a starring role in the Broadway musical *Annie*.

'I always got the feeling they adored each other,' recalled Allan Metter, who directed Parker in *Girls Just Want to Have Fun* the following year (and Robert in *Back to School* the year after that). 'He would come down and hang out with Sarah Jessica. Apparently they were fighting in her trailer, so she would come on to the set to do some happy scene in tears with her mascara running. I remember saying to Downey, "Don't come down here – you're ruining my movie! Stop making her unhappy! She's playing a happy girl this movie.'"

Despite the success of landing a part in *Firstborn*, Robert was still unsettled, frustrated that other parts weren't forthcoming. With only a short film, *Dead Wait*, to name following his appearance in *Firstborn*, he would describe this time as a low point. 'Sarah Jessica Parker called and said, "What are you doing?" I said, "I was just making some quiche. What are you doing?" But I was, like, eating cranberry sauce out of a can.'

Later he added to the *Japan Times*, 'Somewhere or other I read the fiction that I was very successful very early. Untrue. Like everybody, I've had auditions and more auditions and some of the roles I lost, or didn't get, devastated me at the time. Which shows you what life's really like. Don't dwell too long on your failure; it's a form of narcissism and it helps nothing. Just move on. Move along blithely, as Oscar Wilde might have said.'

It was during this period that Robert began to experiment with harder drugs. In keeping with his family's outlook on being open about everything, he would tell Parker everything. 'I was stunned,' she remembered. 'I did not recognise the signs. I did not know the profundity of it. I was innocent in so many ways. I thought, "Well, I will help him." I didn't think that addiction was something that would impose itself on us. I was very wrong.'

Robert still saw nothing wrong with recreational drugs at this time, thinking of them as nothing more than a side note to a party experience. To him it seemed that everyone was doing it. 'My friends and I were out of our minds, absolutely out of control, partying. In New York, eighteen years old, thought we had it together because we were making $1,250 a week. Completely on the road to destruction. I carried all my money around in my pocket. The idea of an accountant never occurred to me. The hand-to-mouth existence of my family was completely my way.'

Robert also began to experiment with an androgynous image, decking himself in laces and frills. 'A lot of my peer group think I'm an eccentric bisexual,' he said at the time. 'That's OK. Being relaxed about sexuality is something you're born with.'

Much later, in a 2000 interview with *Detour* magazine, Robert went into great detail about his sexuality. 'One of my cousins sucked my dick when I was nine. It was for about four seconds and I said I would do it back to him, but I reneged. When I was like fifteen I had something going on with a tranny. It was in New York City at a *Rocky Horror* show. There were all these other Addams Family characters of dubious gender around us. Her name was International Chrysis and I really was sure that she was a white girl with a pussy ... but then there was more. I was there, actually, for the pot, not the surprise member.

'When no girls were around, my best friend in high school and I would make out with each other as a last resort. Let's see, I woke up in a guy's house in New York, who I admired from theatre camp and he was sucking my dick. Did he think that I'd wake up and suddenly find him wildly attractive? I never looked at him the same way. And then there was this guy on a soap who was really cool and he used to have lots of blow and he kissed me with a five o'clock shadow and that didn't work for me. Then there was this hot young director, maybe five years ago, who I found standing behind me in a Royalton hotel robe that had a big boner pushing it up – and that wasn't going to happen. I immediately started calling hookers to come over just to get a buffer between this, uh, potential intrusion.

'My last foray was when one of my best friends came to Italy. I warned him about eating in Rome, that for them a four-star-rated restaurant was like a D-rated greasy spoon in Detroit. He got sick on a piece of fish. I wanted to get blow and so we were heading to a gay bar to look for some and I kissed him out on the street. I was drunk and it just felt right. If I was gay, I'd do it the way Sir Ian McKellen has, in a classy, tasteful way.'

Moving on to the broader topic of sexuality in general, Robert was equally frank. 'It's so crazy that nowadays people have to consider closeting themselves. Because I'm not leading a double life –

because I don't have a quote-unquote documented past – [and] because I'm not using some foot soldier to keep me clamped down from any sort of exposés, I have no reservations about putting to word my thoughts, projections, beliefs. I don't have those fears.

'I think everybody is bisexual. I've acted upon gay situations less than practically every other man I know. As much as I consider myself a sexual person – and not without a fairly rich fantasy life – I'm not very sexually motivated. I'm not sexually addicted or compulsive.

'I'd say twenty-five per cent of the men I know have a serious addiction to sex. The other twenty-five per cent are bisexual, but are in complete and utter vowed silence about it – which is really weird. The other twenty-five per cent are gay. And the other twenty-five per cent are vehemently heterosexual with leather queen undertones.'

More recently Robert has somewhat distanced himself from this androgynous image, saying it was 'manufactured'. 'I didn't have an identity. I was playing around. I expressed it. I grew up in the *Rocky Horror Picture Show* world, where even my butch friends turned out to be androgynous on Saturday night.'

Whatever the truth, it was clear Robert was struggling to make that impact on the screen he was desperate for. Parker was certainly the rock in his life, grounding him as best as she could. But his drug taking was getting out of control and with his big break still eluding him, things were getting desperate. Luckily, help was at hand – at first glance anyway.

Robert was about to receive a phone call that would change his life. However, this development would take back him to LA – and out of the sobering hands of Parker. 'If you come here with character defects that haven't been realised,' Robert would say of LA, 'they are going to come to life.'

4

THE BRAT PACK
HAVE AN OPENING

*'I can't make him toe the line, but
I sure can make him smile'*
SARAH JESSICA PARKER

The phone call was one asking Robert if he wanted a part in *Tuff Turf* – an American drama that was to star James Spader as Morgan, a troubled teenager who moves to LA. There he meets Robert Downey Jr's character Jimmy.

'I was a teenager when I got to LA to do *Tuff Turf*,' Robert remembered. 'I was on the Universal lot. I went to Los Angeles and it was like all my dreams came true. And there were no repercussions. It was the 1980s. And I fit in real well. I'm like the last guy at the party. But I never stopped working. I was making tons of money. I was set up in a relationship with Sarah Jessica Parker and it just seemed like I could do no wrong.'

However, heading to LA meant leaving Parker alone in New York while she filmed a TV after-school special. 'It was difficult,' she said. 'But I wasn't going to say to someone I'd known for six weeks, "Give up the movie!"'

'We miss each other,' Robert would add, 'but we realise that our first priority has to be our careers. Otherwise we wouldn't be any good for each other.'

Talking about his trip to LA for *Tuff Turf*, Robert said, 'I came from New York. I wasn't one of the fellows who grew up in Malibu and their family was in the industry. I'd never had a car, I'd never had the clothes. It's so stupid, but cars, clothes, parties – they were what it was about.'

He hit it off with Spader almost immediately.

'I couldn't believe I was flying first class,' Robert remembered. 'I came out here and was under Jimmy Spader's wing and he said, "Come stay at the Chateau – it's going to be great.' It was there that Robert met Mark Miller, an aspiring screenwriter who was working as a production assistant on the film.

'It was our first movie,' said Miller. 'I was a PA, he was an actor. My job was to watch him and get him to the set on time and things like that.'

They were to form a lasting relationship. Robert helped Miller out as the writer struggled financially. Miller reciprocated by always making sure he was there for Robert when he struggled with legal matters, going as far as to accompany him to court and helping him record a speech from his prison cell to be used at a tribute event for Jodie Foster in 1999.

Another friend during this heady 1980s period was an up-and-coming actor called Josh Richman, who would go on to make a couple of movies with Robert. 'Bob's illness is that he has never known true freedom,' he said. 'Freedom is dictated by boundaries and an oddly beautiful thing about Robert is that he's basically lived without them. His path is not a linear one – you can't compare it to any other person's. Maybe, to Bob, leading what everyone else thinks is a perfect life is not perfect. Maybe Bob doesn't like life like that.'

What *Tuff Turf* also represented for Robert was the start of a pattern that would rear its head several times in his career. In Robert's head, acting came easily for him. He had charisma that the camera catches perfectly and his lazy but high-octane delivery marked him out as a natural. But this ease, coupled with a tendency to be the life and soul of the party, meant that drink and drugs weren't getting in the way of his acting career.

'It was never easy, partying the way that I did, which was as often as I could. But it was do-able. And as long as it was do-able, I wasn't going to stop. So I'm surprised it didn't happen sooner.'

Tuff Turf wasn't a classic movie by any means, but it gave him screen time and it wasn't long before other roles began to come in. He would impress in the supporting but memorable role as 'cool kid' Ian in John Hughes' 1985 comedy *Weird Science*, and briefly saw himself name-checked as one of the Brat Pack.

The Brat Pack became one of the defining 1980s phenomena, and films like *St Elmo's Fire*, *The Breakfast Club*, *Pretty in Pink* and *Less Than Zero* (starring Robert) are seen as some of its defining movies. Who actually made up the Brat Pack is open to endless debate, but the core names include Rob Lowe, Andrew McCarthy, Ally Sheedy, Molly Ringwald, James Spader, Demi Moore and Judd Nelson.

Robert was certainly on the fringes of the pack – he has been mentioned often enough in books and magazines as being something of an honorary member – but Robert himself distanced himself from this perceived clique. 'I can completely and happily be not in the loop of my peer group,' he said. 'I don't go to their houses. I don't know where they go, they don't know where I go.'

Written by Hughes in two days, *Weird Science* told the story of two 15-year-old boys who decided to create the ultimate woman using a computer programme. It made a star out of Kelly LeBrock and it was while filming *Weird Science* that Robert met Anthony Michael Hall, one of Hollywood's biggest rising stars who was playing one of the nerdy lead roles.

At the audition, Robert remembered walking into

John Hughes' office to see Hall fiddling about with the director's stereo system. 'It was like running into Spencer Tracy or something,' Robert recalled. 'It was like seeing a movie star. Michael came in and watched us read and he kind of looked at me, like, "I'm going to tell John to get you this job." I remember that Sarah was in the car outside waiting for me and I said, "I think I got this job."'

During the making of the film, Robert became better known for a rather distasteful habit than for his acting ability. 'I was the serial dumper,' he admitted. 'I defecated in [Kelly LeBrock]'s trailer, much to the chagrin of [fellow stars] Bill Paxton and Robert Rusler. It was a real bad scene. [Producer] Joel Silver freaked. I never admitted it. Joel said, "Downey, did you do it?" And I said, "I wish I had." Because I'd been threatening everyone that if they didn't treat me right, I was going to take a dump in their trailer, or that I'd go take a shit in Joel's office on his desk or something.

'It was the serial dump,' he admitted. 'Me and Anthony Michael Hall scared the shit out of security guards doing doughnuts in the parking lot.'

It was Robert at his self-destructive worst. Here he was landing a supporting role in a major movie and he was doing his best to get himself fired. But in what would be a trait that would rear its head countless times in Robert's career, he would often get away with it. Perhaps it was his lovable roguish charm, but directors clearly seemed to indulge him. Even the legendary Silver wasn't immune to Robert's charms. Not only would he *not* fire Robert from *Weird Science*, he would play a huge part in Robert's comeback almost 20 years later.

Weird Science would prove to be one of Hughes' rare commercial misfires, but it was a film close to Robert's heart. 'I love comedy,' he would say later. 'I have this genius idea that no one else is interested in. I think we should remake *Weird Science* twenty years later. Anthony Michael Hall works for a company and he's a total loser and my girl, he wants to reanimate, because he has a secret admirer thing for my wife so he reanimates her. That would make $300 million.'

Following *Weird Science*, Robert starred in the seven-hour TV mini-series *Mussolini: The Untold Story*, in which he played Bruno, the second son of the Italian fascist dictator (George C Scott). 'To prepare for it, all I did was read the script and drink cappuccino,' Robert quipped.

'When I went in to audition for *Mussolini: The Untold Story*, I still had purple dye in my hair from *Weird Science* and they're like, "Oh, I... I don't think so." And I was like, "Yeah, right, guys." And then I read one scene and they said, "Oh, great. Great. That was really great! Read the next one.' I was like, "Nah, I gotta go." My vibe told me get out of there and make them think. So I left and they called that day – "Oh, you were so magical."

'It doesn't matter whether or not you can act. If you can go into a room and make these sweaters want to have you around for six or eight weeks, that's what'll really get you a job.'

Filming took place in communist Yugoslavia, which he would describe as 'horrible', but he enjoyed working with the veteran Scott. 'You think about the guy who's been in *Patton* and all those fucking amazing movies having to be who he is in the shittiest fucking possible country to shoot in. We were all unhappy there. I'm not saying that he really even liked me, but didn't dislike me, which is why he might have taken any interest at all in me.'

It was certainly an eventful shoot, with one incident seeing Robert nearly cut to pieces. 'We were shooting George's close-up and I started running towards these planes. Some people get mesmerised by the turning blades. I almost ran right into this fucking propeller. I'll always send Gabriel Byrne a Christmas card because he saved my life. He pushed me out of the way of this thing. And I was suddenly down on the ground and said, "Jesus Christ, it made sense to me to run through that. It seemed my mark was on the other side of it." And George Scott just said, "Cut! You stupid prick. Always look where you're going! What the fuck are you doing? Goddamn it!" He was so pissed off that I'd almost made him have to watch me die on his close-ups. But it was general concern too. It was cool. I did it again for attention.

'Another thing about George – more important than anything else – was that he kicked everybody's ass in that country in chess. People were flying in from all over. He was like, "Check." That was really great to see. And he wasn't ever really paying attention when he was doing it.'

Next up for Robert was something of a career shift. He was asked to be a regular on the acclaimed weekly US show *Saturday Night Live*. This enduring comedy show, which is still going, had introduced the likes of Dan Aykroyd, Bill Murray, Chevy Chase and Eddie Murphy to a worldwide audience, thanks to founder Lorne Michaels scouring the comedy clubs to find the freshest talent.

Michaels had only intended to take a few months off after the 1980 season, but his absence lasted all of five years. Now, as he returned to the show, Michaels would insist on a cast spring clean – regulars like Billy Crystal and Martin Short were becoming bigger than the weekly guest stars. But instead of going to the comedy clubs as he had before, Michaels turned to veterans like Randy Quaid and rising comedy stars on the screen. As Tom Hanks (one of the regular guest stars on the show) said, 'It was a sort of cobbled-together cast. Lorne put it together in six weeks.'

Nevertheless it was a huge honour to be asked to be

one of the regular performers on the show, and again it was down to Anthony Michael Hall, Robert's friend and co-star in *Weird Science*, that he got the job.

'We were always talking about wanting to do something,' Robert explained, 'The show was re-forming, Lorne Michaels was coming back and Michael got excited about it. They were on Anthony Michael Hall's dick to get him on the show. And so he negotiated some ridiculous contract and then also said, "Well, Robert Downey has to be on the show, too."'

So Robert went to the audition but instead of the handful of people he was expecting, the judges turned out to be 'all of NBC'. Undaunted, Robert went in. 'I was wearing a T-shirt. I took my T-shirt off and threw it on my head and started doing this character – my imitation of this guy that I'd seen at a club. This Iranian guy was drunk and didn't know the language well and he was talking shit to this guy, saying, "Hey, man – you don't know who I am. You'll kick my ass." I was like, "No – it's, '*I'll* kick *your* ass.'" So I went in and started doing this Iranian for the audition and they started laughing and they started hiring me.'

Robert's 18 weeks on *Saturday Night Live* were a heady time for the young actor. 'Live TV is the ultimate medium,' he has said. "Two hundred of your best friends in the audience, five cameras in your face, not enough time to get it together and thirty million people watching.' It looked like being a dream come true when a super-hot pop star by the name of

Madonna was lined up as the first guest, Robert was allocated former *SNL* hero John Belushi's dressing room and unusual requests like bunk beds with NFL sheets were met with replies of, 'Yes, sir, of course, sir.'

However, it wasn't a particularly fruitful time in *Saturday Night Live*'s history. In fact, the season including Robert is seen as one of the rare low points in the show's history.

Writers found it hard to come up with the right material for the eccentric group. One of them, Tom Schiller (who had returned to the show with Michaels), told authors Tom Shales and Andrew James Miller in their fascinating book *Live From New York*, 'In the early days I was pretty much left alone. I could go into a meeting and say, "I want to do a thing with John Belushi as an old guy – he does this and that." And then they'd say, "Great! Do it." I'd write a script and go around and show it to people.

'But later it became difficult. After the five-year gap, I went back and worked there a little bit and it was murder. They assigned some young writer to work with me and it was bad. They had more checks and balances and that was bad. Somebody said Lorne had become the corporate person that he used to make fun of. It became more of a business. Suddenly there was a guy with a clipboard walking around while you were writing your sketches and stuff, making sure you were working.

'When the show first started, no one knew what

was going on and there was a wonderful flux period, which was incredibly creative. We were more individuals in the early days. Then in 1985, the show had coalesced and you found you were just an interchangeable part. Not that the drugs were good, but there was no more drugs. It was clean. It wasn't as rambunctious – that's the word.'

It may have been a clean and drug-free environment for the writers, but it certainly wasn't for Robert. He and Hall were kindred spirits, both young and keen partygoers. 'Michael was probably the most amazing pussy wizard in history,' Robert said. 'And if you were anywhere near him, you were having fun. He's seventeen years old and there are gorgeous girls everywhere. I was twenty, so I'm barely making it there on Monday to meet the new host, you know.'

The first show would prove to be one that summed up that season of *SNL*. 'We opened the season with Madonna hosting the show and there was tremendous hype,' recalled writer James Downey (no relation). 'It was an offensive, dreadful show. I don't know how many shows there've been – more than five hundred. I would say the Madonna show has got to be considered one of the top five – I mean, in an entirely negative way. It really crippled the season from the get-go, particularly since there were a lot of people anxious to see that new group of actors fail. That first show was like an albatross for us. Years later people would still say, "I haven't watched the show since that

Madonna thing."'

The main problem was that, being a live show packed with sketches, SNL had to be fast paced. But Madonna did not easily fit the format and she wasn't yet that experienced. As cast member Damon Wayans recalled, 'She had never done this before.'

That episode was a huge ratings hit but, as James Downey ruefully admitted, 'The bad news is, a lot of people were watching.'

NBC executive Dick Ebersol said in the book *Live From New York*, 'I think Lorne's first year back in 1985 was very dark. It was a very dark year. It was the roughest season Lorne ever had doing the show and everybody came out of the woodwork to attack. It was the first time he'd ever been subject to that *Saturday Night Dead* stuff.'

Hall agreed that it was one of the most forgettable seasons in the show's history. 'I certainly didn't make a major impact on the show like a lot of people did. But just to be a part of it from my standpoint was amazing. It's far and away the most competitive environment I've ever worked in. Some guy who was based in the West, a fan of the show, would send me tapes of selected sketches where it was so blatantly obvious that I was reading cue cards. He had time to do an edited version of, like, my worst cue card readings, the ones that were most blatant. It didn't bother me – I thought it was hilarious.'

After the season ended, only a handful of the cast

members would be asked back. Showbiz manager Bernie Brillstein said, 'Robert was one of the people [Michaels] really wanted and it wasn't a terrible idea, but it wasn't a good idea either, in retrospect. It just didn't work. And there were a few problems among the cast – I mean alcohol and drugs and whatever. It wasn't good.'

Robert remembered Lorne Michaels saying, '"Don't make me look bad." You know? It's really heavy. After I left, after that first season, it got better. I don't mean by the fact that I left.'

While he was filming *Saturday Night Live*, Robert was also making the 1986 comedy movie *Back to School*. 'So I'd fly back to Los Angeles for a couple of days during the week to shoot the movie and then fly back and, "Live, From New York, It's a Tired Young Man!"'

But Robert's talents at hiding his partying and drug taking weren't as honed as he would like people to believe. According to the movie's director Alan Metter, 'I suspect that sometimes he was working stoned.

'In the editing room, I manicured his performances. I really dug deep. I'm not saying he stunk in the movie – he didn't – but it's possible he didn't have the skills he had later. Or maybe he learned a lesson on my picture? I doubt he'd admit that.'

As an example, Metter added, 'We were supposed to be filming a scene that featured him and he didn't show up on the set. We had his friends and his father and the police and everybody looking for him, while my eighty-man crew were sitting around reading newspapers. I had my camera operator sitting on the dolly with the *LA Times* open and we were paying him.

'[Robert] finally showed up in the afternoon and he had been up all night. We were filming in a little dorm room and Downey fell asleep on one of the beds. So I had the grips get gaffer tape and, like in *Gulliver's Travels*, they used a hundred or so strips of tape and we taped him to the floor. He woke up and couldn't move. That was my payback.'

However, Keith Gordon, who also starred in the film, insists that he never saw Robert take drugs. '[He] was like an energetic puppy,' he recalled. 'He was a wacky kid. He's one of the most lovable people you'll ever meet. You want to mother and father him. He broadcasts a certain amount of innate goodness and he's sweet and vulnerable.'

Despite Metter's admission that he struggled with Robert's performance at times on *Back to School*, Robert would say that the director 'let me go wild a couple of times, which no one else has done. That was fun.

'My hair. I was such a nerd – I thought the higher my hair, the more handsome I was. It gives me a chance to get all of this mugging out of my system once and for all. I got pretty Stan Laurel at times.'

Metter said, 'We had a good script, written by

Harold Ramis. Robert was most comfortable when he was improvising. When we got into the written dialogue, he tended to stiffen up a little bit. I found he was frustrating to work with as a director because I saw his best performances in the blocking and rehearsals and, by the time I rolled the camera, he was kind of just going through the motions. I actually started rolling the camera early. For me, I would much rather have a great performance modestly lit, than a poor performance perfectly lit. But I was constantly duelling with my DOP about rolling the camera on Downey early.'

He would tell the actor about his performances but, according to Metter, he just shrugged his shoulders. 'What could he say? He never argued that the stuff you're getting is better than the rehearsal, because he knew it too.

'That's the worst part of directing. What you want is, "I caught magic." But the performances I filmed were never as exciting as stuff I saw in rehearsal. I can hear myself telling him many times on that movie to do it like he did in rehearsals, but we never seemed to get back to it.

'And that sort of wore me down, so that my memory of working with him – and don't forget I wasn't working with the great Robert Downey, I was working with Robert Downey the actor – it was always a little disappointing.'

Robert's memories of that time were, 'Rent-a-cars,

flying back and forth, doing *Saturday Night Live*, partying – a lot of partying – with everyone and anyone. It was madness. That's what it really was. Pure madness. My relationship with Sarah Jessica Parker stayed, though. She kept me rooted through that whole period. But I consider myself really lucky to have gotten through it with any sort of career and a working respiratory system.'

Talking about the drugs, Parker said later, 'I believed I was the person holding him together. In every good and bad way I enabled him to get up in the morning and show up for work. If he did not, I was there to cover for him, find him, clean him up and get him to the set or theatre. The machinations of all that are the worst. You are not even in a romantic relationship any more. It is like a parent–child thing.'

As Robert admitted, 'Not having that affliction herself, it was just confounding for her. But we had a love for each other that overcame all of that and there was a surprisingly high percentage of normal days as well.'

Chris Bell, Robert's friend from his early school days, remembered seeing him during that time, after Robert had called him out of the blue. He told author Ben Falk, 'At that time he'd just finished his stint on *Saturday Night Live* and he was definitely the star. He already had a string of movies and was definitely successful, but he was still the same guy. There's a very private side to him.

'I think most of his friends only got to know this one side of him that was funny, personable, very nice. I'm not suggesting he has a dark side but there is a very private side – we didn't talk about his family, even his dad, other than the funny things. I'm sure he went through a lot of angst with his parents and that whole broken family situation but I don't think he ever shared that with too many people, if anyone. When I see him on television, that really captures the way I remember him – he'd always put on voices, he's always put on characters, he didn't take things too seriously.

'He was always able to maintain a great love of life but I can also see that he obviously had his demons. He would overcompensate because, when I think about the drugs, that to me indicates there was something missing.'

5

ROBERT TAKES
THE LEAD

*'I was playing this junkie and the character was an
exaggeration of myself. Then things changed and, in some
ways, I became an exaggeration of the character. That
lasted far longer than it needed to'*
ROBERT DOWNEY JR

Despite Robert's hyperactive socialising, he and
Sarah Jessica Parker still managed to live a
relatively normal domestic life with homes in both
New York and LA. In California their house was the
one where Charlie Chaplin had lived: they would
live there with their Persian cats called Mr Smith
and Scout.

'Thing were going well,' Robert recalled. 'When I
wasn't working, I was going to Red Square, going out
to clubs all the time.' Offers of work were flooding in
and he believed that, as long as he could still perform

to a reasonable standard, he didn't see why he should curb his partying lifestyle. 'That wasn't a good thing to cultivate,' he would recognise later.

Things were certainly looking up in his career. Writer-director James Toback was looking for his lead actor for his film *The Pick-Up Artist*, a romantic comedy about a womaniser who falls for a mobster's daughter. Robert might have been a hit with the ladies, but he insists he has never been one to go up to a girl and do the 'Hey, how about me and you' kind of thing. But what he was, was charming. He seduced Toback almost instantly at the audition, laying down on the floor and just 'saying whatever I felt like saying'.

'He walked into my office at Fox on 57th Street,' Toback recalled, 'and literally a minute after we started talking, I said, "By the way, you want to play the lead in this movie?" And he said, "Sure." He made you like him immensely without trying.'

Toback added later, 'He was twenty, with slight gaps between his teeth, a ready, wild laugh, mischievous dark eyes, a graceful sense of movement and a compact but insufficiently toned frame. He was also a witty, fast talker, which was essential for the role. I gave him the part – his first substantial role – after one meeting. No screen test, no reading. I hoped my irrational leap of faith would create confidence in him, which was the one quality I suspected he might hold in short supply.'

For Robert, *The Pick-Up Artist* was finally his big

chance to break out from his supporting roles and become the leading man. He would have to go on a diet for the film – 'Two pastas a day, a lot of liquids, some bran, some yoghurt. It's really incredibly boring' – but he would get to star alongside Molly Ringwald, one of the 1980s cinema sweethearts. Robert was taken aback by how much he learned from working with her.

'She's very intelligent,' he said. 'She's very eager. I was surprised at the energy she takes in educating herself. She's always reading. And she's a smart businesswoman. In *The Pick-Up Artist* we were doing a scene where she's walking away from me and she drops a bottle of Maalox [antacid]. I have to pick it up before she can get it and say, "God, is there something wrong with your stomach?"

'There's usually this understood thing between actors that if something has to happen in a scene, we help each other make it happen. But while we were doing it, she dropped the Maalox and I went to pick it up. But she picked it up before I did and the scene was over. What she was saying was, "Listen, if you're really going to be in the moment, you've got to get it before I can." It was just a really ballsy thing to do. It was probably one of the more important lessons I learned, especially because it's so easy to be desensitised and wish to be in the station wagon going home.'

Toback was wowed by Downey's performance, saying, 'His mind is capable of going into just about any channel at any minute. Even Robert doesn't know who he's going to be from one moment to another.'

His decision to make Robert his leading man in *The Pick-Up Artist* was given instant vindication when legendary film critic Pauline Kael wrote, 'Downey, whose soul is floppy eared, gives the movie a fairy-tale sunniness.'

Unfortunately for Robert, *The Pick-Up Artist* flopped at the box office – something that irked him, along with press accusations that the film's attitude to womanising was morally irresponsible. 'People kept asking me that question,' he said later. 'All I wanted to do was promote *The Pick-Up Artist* and the press kept asking me about exalted legal and moral issues. I'm like, "Come on, man – I just hope it does well at the box office." Of course it's a sexually irresponsible film, but if AIDS had happened six months later, maybe the film would have made more than six bucks.'

Still, it was great experience for Robert and, while his next film would see him be part of an ensemble rather than a leading man, *Less Than Zero* would be the movie that made everyone sit up and take notice. Unfortunately, it would also provide a tragic foreshadowing of the addictions and struggles that would take hold of him. It's no surprise that he called the role the 'ghost of Christmas future'.

Loosely based on the novel by Bret Easton Ellis, the film looks at freshman student Clay (Andrew

McCarthy), who returns to his wealthy but broken family in Beverly Hills to find his best friend Julian (Robert) sinking further and further into drug use. As Julian's addiction deepens, his life spirals out of control.

'Two minutes after he walked in, before he even read, I knew he was right,' said director Marek Kanievska about casting him in *Less Than Zero*. 'Robert gives you 360 degrees. You just have to keep it in check and give it focus. I love Robert as an actor because he constantly takes risks.'

It was the first time Robert had been asked to create a character from scratch – one that wouldn't just rely on his natural enthusiasm and an easy laugh. 'I took the part because this kind of guy hasn't really been done before on film – a potential artist who slips really low,' he said. 'There's a lot of humour in the film, but overall it's pretty grim. It's most disturbing … I just figured I'd better get into it and go for it. I tried not to think what an extreme person Julian was.

'I think a lot of actors were turned off it because Julian has bisexual encounters, but you can't be paranoid about what people are going to think. I was getting dangerously close to that. I thought I might have a good shot. Because I really couldn't see many of my peers being able to handle playing a crack-whore. I was so fucking happy I got cast. I figured any actor who is smart and semi-fearless would know that this is a great role.'

Less Than Zero was not an easy film for the studio bosses to market – just endless scenes of rich kids taking drugs and having sex. The film also showed several big changes from the book – most notably the inclusion of an anti-drug message and the changing of Clay's sexuality. He is bisexual in the book, but that was excised from the film by 20th Century Fox bosses, who were keen to appeal to heartthrob McCarthy's teen fan base.

Aware now of Robert's many rehab visits and drug encounters, people might look at *Less Than Zero* and think that he was less acting and more re-enacting his life at this time, but *Less Than Zero* showcased Robert as one to watch. Most people had no idea how much he was blurring the lines between fiction and reality, apart from those who knew him well.

Jami Gertz, who plays the love interest in the movie, said, '*Less Than Zero* was a low point in his life. The scenes were so true to life. It was all happening to him. You had the feeling, "Is this guy going to make it?" Is what happens to Julian going to happen to Robert?'

Robert would concede later, 'I suppose things did change for me when I was making that film. Up until that point in my life, I had just partied on weekends, like a lot of people, but the character I was playing in *Less Than Zero* was a full-on junkie and that began to reflect what was going on in my personal life.

'Until that movie, I took my drugs after work and

on the weekends. Maybe I'd turn up hungover on the set, but no more so than the stuntman. That changed on *Less Than Zero*. I was playing this junkie faggot guy and, for me, the role was like the ghost of Christmas future. The character was an exaggeration of myself. Then things changed and, in some ways, I became an exaggeration of the character. That lasted far longer than it needed to last.'

Talking about the drug addiction that took hold, he told *Esquire* magazine in 2009, 'That first time it was opium. The second time it looked like opium. Looked the same, smelled the same, a little dirtier, not quite as pristine a buzz and by the time three weeks later, when I woke up, thought I had the flu and took a hit on it, I looked up and said, "Great. So now we're junkies. This is fucking great."

'I was always the guy who was like, "No heroin. No crack." But it doesn't matter if you go ten years without doing it. Because on that 3,651st day, it's your turn.'

Despite the goings-on behind the camera, Robert was justifiably proud of the film. 'People leaving the theatre are not going to feel so much entertained as if they'd been hit in the solar plexus with something real, something that is timely and poignant,' he said. 'Yet there's a lot of love in it among the three main characters, clouded love though it may be. I think audiences will sense three real, caring relationships. A lot of people may be angered by it, but others are going to say, "God, that's me," or, "That's my brother or a potential me." It's an important film and I really feel lucky to be a part of it.'

During test screenings of the film, however, the young audience were negative towards Robert's character, saying he wasn't likeable enough – resulting in the addition of a graduation flashback scene to show the trio in a lighter light.

'They hated Downey's character,' said producer Scott Rudin. 'There has been a tremendous conservative change in young audiences since the book was written in 1984. Their fantasy used to be great sexual experimentation. Now it is to live in a great apartment, have a great boyfriend and wear great clothes.'

The reviews of *Less Than Zero* were decidedly mixed, with several nonplussed critics bemoaning a sanitised version of the Ellis novel. Robert, however, was hailed for his performance, with the *New York Times* calling it 'desperately moving', Leonard Maltin calling him 'exceptional' and the *Chicago Sun-Times* saying his 'acting is so real, so subtle and so observant that it's scary'.

Not everyone was pleased with the movie, however. 'I don't know anyone who was happy with it,' said author Ellis. 'The director wasn't happy with it and it was this compromised movie for many, many reasons. I don't think it began that way – I think that Scott Rudin and Barry Diller, who were the ones who brought it to 20th Century Fox, had a very different movie in mind. I think when there was the regime change at the studio with Leonard Goldberg taking over, who was a family man who had kids, it became a different beast. I grew up around Hollywood and I had no real desire to see the book made into a movie. I thought, "Well, we'll take the money and ninety-eight per cent of all books optioned never make it to the screen, so…"'

It wasn't long, however, before Robert realised just how important the movie could be to people who saw it. 'I was in Georgia and this lady came up to me shaking and said, "I saw you in *Less Than Zero*." I felt like saying, "Why are you shaking? You're every bit as special as I am." But I was in a pissed-off mood and I didn't want to be a prick, so I said my usual, "Thanks a lot," and started to walk away. Then she said, "Two of my friends went into rehab after seeing you in that movie." I got chills up and down my spine and thought, "Fuck, now I know why I do what I do."'

The film and his performance also touched his girlfriend, who marvelled at his ability. Talking himself more about Parker, he raved, 'There's no competition between us. I do my thing and she does hers. It's great to see someone grow. When I did *Less Than Zero*, she said, "I can't believe I live with you. I really think you're great at what you do." And I saw her in *A Year in the Life* or the TV show she did,

Life Under Water, and I fell in love with her a hundred times more – because it was like I wanted the girl that I saw in the movie to be my girlfriend and she already was!'

Critical opinion seems to be kinder for *Less Than Zero* nowadays: in 2008 it made the list of The 25 Best LA films of the past 25 years in the *LA Times*. The newspaper said, 'With its neon-bathed shots of Melrose Avenue, decadent nightclub set-pieces and scenes plotted around the turquoise brilliance of swimming pools at night, *Less Than Zero* viscerally evokes the Big Empty – the hedonism, superficiality and laissez-faire nihilism – of 1980s LA. Adapted from Bret Easton Ellis' 1985 bestseller, the film functions as a Reagan-era anti-drug screed aimed at the MTV generation. It stars a subset of the Brat Pack – Andrew McCarthy, Jami Gertz and a kinetic, pre-rehab Robert Downey Jr – as a trio of young, rich burn-outs drifting through the city's nightscape in a haze of cocaine and anomie.'

Even Ellis, who initially stated that he hated the film, says he has accepted it and warmed to it now. 'I now like *Less Than Zero*. I have gotten very sentimental about it – it bears no resemblance to the book – but it did capture a certain youth culture during that decade that no other movie caught – LA youth culture in 1985, 1986, 1987 in a stunningly beautiful way. The photography was amazing. But it is a miscast movie, though, except for Downey and

Spader, and the writing and directing was off, but visually I loved it.'

Ellis has written a sequel to *Less Than Zero*, entitled *Imperial Bedrooms*, and hopes that it will form a sequel on the big screen too. Despite Robert's character dying at the end of the film, Ellis still thinks he could appear in the sequel. 'The cast is still around, so it would be really funny to see. And this book is pretty dramatic, in terms of how complicated the relationships have gotten in the last twenty years.

'I first thought [they'd be dead] when I started thinking about it; when I began to outline the book and figure out who's going to be around and who's not – some of the main people are going to be OK. There was some supporting cast that I realised was expendable – you knew something bad was going to happen to them. But the leads? Yeah, they kind of stuck around.

'Now that I'm finally done with the book I'm thinking, "God, what if Fox wants to do this as a film?" Because Fox did the original and I think there's a rights issue involved… I think it would be a great idea. We'll see.'

But would it be a place that Robert would ever revisit?

'Something happened to my psyche or spirituality while I was filming *Less Than Zero*,' he said. 'I mean, you start digging into your duffel bag that's filled with all of your repressed ideas. Maybe there's a family

73

crisis, but you think, "I've got to put this in the back of my head because I've got other things to think about." Until finally there's this pile of dirty mismatched socks at the bottom. I started to mentally pick them out and fluff and fold them.'

6

ROBERT THE
FILM STAR

*'I'd like to be in one of those films where
at the end you go, "Yeah!"'*
ROBERT DOWNEY JR

Following his personal success in *Less Than Zero*, the world should have been Robert's oyster. However, his drug addiction was taking an increasing hold on him and, coupled with a string of bizarre role choices and bad luck at the box office, his leading-man lure was beginning to fade.

One of those films would see Robert reunite with Anthony Michael Hall for 1988's *Johnny Be Good*, a coming-of-age comedy that saw him play Leo, the friend of Hall's promising high-school quarterback. 'They hated me in *Johnny Be Good*. The *Los Angeles Times* crucified me. They said I sounded like Pee-wee Herman emerging from a coma. I'm not sure I've been in a real good movie. It'd be nice to try that. I'd like, you know, to be in one of those films where at the end you go, "Yeah!"'

'Lately,' he added, 'I think the most important thing for me as an actor is to keep working. I want to keep working. I want to keep learning. I'm in a position to start saying no to projects. It's too easy to just keep picking scripts that are very me and something that's so easy for me to do. Now I look for a role that I wouldn't think I can play right off the bat. What it comes down to is that I want to do roles I can learn from.'

So perhaps it shouldn't have come as a surprise that his next role would be in his father's comedy *Rented Lips*. 'I play a porno star named Wolf Dangler,' said Robert, 'with fishnet underwear and boots, who thinks he's Marlon Brando. That was the greatest experience I've ever had in a film, because I could do what I wanted. I love screaming and yelling and goofing off and hamming it up.'

Talking about working with his dad for the first since he was a young child, he said, 'If I could go into directing, I could learn a lot from him. Working with him on *Rented Lips* was great because he always called me by my character's name. He went out of his way to make sure that there was were no concessions made to me because I was his son.

'He'd let me sing songs and do improvs. It makes me feel good that he's proud of me. I think he's proud that I'm not as stereotypical as I easily could have been.'

Robert also worked on a campaign called Vote 88, alongside Sarah Jessica Parker. The idea was to use star appeal to encourage people to vote in that year's Presidential election.

'When we did the Vote 88 thing, most people who came out weren't even of age to vote and it didn't really seem like so much of an educational consciousness, or anything. Of course, some people were there, just holding up posters of films you'd been in or whatever, but they're going to hear words and they're going to make up their own choices anyway. And a lot of them are going to go back to a conservative household or whatever, but at least those questions are being raised, at least there're options to make the choices and that information is, in a way, experience.

'See, I'm a high-school drop-out. I need to say that because, on any of these issues, I'm just learning as I go along. And so, say for abortion, inherently I know that it's unconstitutional to take that choice away. So for me, I feel that I can stand on that issue but, at the same time, I know that I listen to the other side. I don't want to be someone who's just like uninformed but passionate. To me, it's really about becoming informed.'

That same year he would also star in the Vietnam War drama *1969*, alongside Kiefer Sutherland. One of the film's producers, Dan Grodnik, said, 'We made a wish list and Downey and Sutherland were at the top. Robert's gonna be a big star. He's got the face, he's got the talent and he's got the style.'

The movie tells the story of two small-town college friends who oppose the war, even though this leads to a family split. Robert accepted his role without reading the script, mainly because of Sutherland's agreement to do the movie. 'Kiefer's really smart,' Robert said. 'He doesn't make a lot of mistakes and I trust his judgement. He's always said, "Man, whatever happened to Redford and Newman? We need some teams." It's like I'm being surrounded by these motivators and I can definitely be a motivating person too, but I kind of need sparks around me.'

It couldn't have hurt that Sutherland was 'one of the funniest wild men I've ever met'.

When they'd finished the movie, however, Robert must have wished he'd read the script before agreeing to star in it. Still, if he wasn't making the films he was desperate to make, his relationship with Parker was still going strong.

'I'd prefer to be outstanding in a great film but, until then, my cats are fed and I'm just happy to be working.

'One can be so insecure as an actor. If I hadn't met Sarah, I don't think I would have gotten a lot of the jobs that I did. Sarah has made me more practical. She got me an accountant and made me open a bank account. The reason you go out is to find somebody with whom you can live comfortably. I don't think I need to look any further.'

Her steadying influence was clearly important to him as he began to grasp for the first time what a true relationship is. 'It's a funny phrase, "taking someone for granted",' he said. 'It's something you're not supposed to do. Yet you *can* take primary aspects of what you need from a relationship for granted: that this person knows you better than your mom does, that you can trust her to mirror things to you that you're blind in.

'I'm really starting to gain an understanding of what a relationship is. That shifting of two people to a third thing – not me, not you, but us – that concept of a sacrificing toward an intangible, higher good. "Us" is magical.'

'We literally grew up together,' Parker added, 'so we know one another so well. If he's exposed to success or beautiful leading ladies – the things that make a lot of people stray – we can work through that because we love one another and want to be together.'

Said Robert, 'I looked at her today and she had her hair pulled back and was wearing these riding pants and a sweatshirt and she was like someone's *wife*. She looked like a woman. And suddenly this belief structure I have – which is that we're both young, and isn't it wild that we found each other in all the insanity and we're trying to play house, but we're not really – suddenly that got pushed aside and I realised that, in finding her own path, Sarah's really become what I always wanted.

'I misinterpreted marriage until recently. It was what was continually going wrong all around me. With my parents, I thought, "They'll never break up." Then they did. So I had these old tapes in my head about what marriage meant. And now I think that, whether or not we actually do it, after you've been with someone a certain amount of time, it happens – a marriage of selves.'

Robert would give Parker a 'kind of a hanging-out-together ring'.

'I'm really happy with Sarah and I don't want to ruin it by planning too far ahead. But the way I feel now, marriage looks like we're headed ... it's also like someone you went to the army with and you've grown up together. It takes work to be in a relationship. You've got to wake up every day and decide that you still want to be with that person. You'll always have love for this person but it's not up to some outside force to bring the magic into your relationship. It's up to you.'

The next film up for Robert was 1969's *True Believer* – a crime drama loosely based on a series of articles by journalist KW Lee about an Asian immigrant convicted of a gangland murder in San Francisco. Directed by Joseph Ruben, *True Believer* would see Robert play an idealistic, fresh-faced young legal clerk who partners James Wood's burnt-out lawyer.

'[Robert has a] combination of sweetness and innocence, with a sort of edgy quality,' said Ruben. 'I cast Downey because he's got this current going on that's fascinating to watch. He came in the first day of rehearsal with an interesting haircut and these punk glasses unlike anything you've ever seen. And I thought, "That's exactly it – that's exactly the character." Jimmy [Woods] calls him Binky; he's constantly saying, "Binky is too cute – I can't be in a movie with anyone this cute." Downey is funny because he's got a tremendous sweetness to him, but got sort of a sly side too. He's up to more than what he lets on.'

Talking about the film's theme of tackling injustice, Woods said, 'We used to go out in masses and march in the street – and it didn't do very much. Today a few guys take somebody to court and it starts to make a dent. Dramatically, it makes sense for a guy to lose faith and have a Binkster [Robert] come along and all of a sudden give some fuel to that fire that's still smouldering but almost out.

'At first it started out as a guy and his henchman. But I think it's more interesting to have a real Butch-and-Sundance routine and that's what Bob and I developed, and a lot of that came out of our friendship. I think Bob is the finest of the young actors. He really has that magic gift – he's a real natural. You either can do it or you can't and if you can it's a matter of how much fun it is between takes.

The Binkmeister and I never think about anything – we just do it. I think I'm gonna adopt Bob. Adopt-a-Bink, it's a new programme!

'You know the feeling when you see a cute little puppy and sense it's going to grow up to be this champion German Shepherd?' he added. 'That's how I feel about Downey. It's fun to see him now in that awkward stage and to know he will be one of the great talents of the next decade.'

The admiration was mutual. 'First of all,' Robert said, 'I liked the film just because I love working with James Woods, because he's so fucking great. You learn a lot while you're hanging out with him, but you wonder why he is so adamant that certain things be a certain way. And then you look back and you understand.

'Between takes today, he said, "I'm going to miss you, Bink. Better keep in touch with me – this thing's meant for a sequel." And then as soon as he hears "Action!" he's into just focusing and giving one thousand per cent. It's kind of the same way I work, so it's great to have this guy confirm my belief that one legitimate approach to acting is knowing what you're doing, knowing the actions, having your shit together and then letting it go and turning it on.'

Explaining his new nickname, Robert said, 'It's because he thought I was a preppy. Or because he said that I wore more silk than it took to land all the troops at Normandy. He would always make fun of me because I'd come to the set in a suit at seven am just because I bought all this shit and wanted to wear it. So he thought I was foppish and he called me Binky. Pretty soon I'd go for lunch and they'd say, '"What do you want today, Binky?" It was one of those Preppy Handbook appropriate male names. But I'm just happy because it means he likes me.

'To me, I look back and count how many times I was stricken to the floor with laughter... Well, we were doing a scene together and I was right on the edge of not acting but really making something happen, you know? It's like trying to really make something spontaneous or great happen. I was saying my lines and he was just looking at me, kind of like, "You're getting there. You're getting there." And then I laughed because it was like masturbating.

'He got this weird look and cocked his head a little bit to the side and he just reached over and fucking cracked me right in the middle of the take. If it hadn't been him, or if the timing hadn't been right, I would have said, "What the fuck are you doing?" But he's so smart, he slapped me on the side of my face that wasn't to the camera and he slapped me on my neck instead of on my face so a big red mark wouldn't show up. He even thought that out.'

But whatever their personal chemistry, their partnership in the movie was a mismatch. Film critic Roger Ebert, despite being a fan of Downey Jr, felt

Robert had struggled to keep up with the frantic energy of James Wood.

Still, after *True Believer*, Robert was now making more money than he had ever dreamed of. His colleagues, however, were worried about his spending habits.

Robert explained, 'When I was making $40 a shift as a busboy, I had all I needed. There is something about making tons of money that makes you spend tons of money, and all of a sudden you never wash your own car, you don't make your own bed. But it's all for a price.

That year would also see Robert star in the reincarnation comedy *Chances Are* alongside Cybill Shepherd. She 'taught me to take my time', Robert said. 'I got so used to playing characters who talk fast. In movies they take so much time setting up shots and stuff and I understand – they're doing their thing. Some DPs take an hour to light a cigarette. It's OK to take your time. I'm not saying it's all right to be self-indulgent, but that's what you're there for, and sometimes you feel so hurried. Everything's hurried so that you can go around and wait until they're ready... Cybill Shepherd is cool.

'It's a nice film, he's a nice guy and he's the most accessible character I've played. Now you'll think I'm the person who's in *Chances Are*, which is nice because he's a nice guy.'

In fact, Robert had nearly lost out on the part, with

the producers having to convince the studio bosses to cast him in the role. It seemed he was acquiring something of a reputation for being difficult on set – indeed, the first day of rehearsals saw him turn up late. However, a chastened Robert would apologise, promising that it wouldn't happen again during the film.

Chances Are producer Mike Lobell remarked, 'I don't think he'd ever been in a successful movie. He'd done a lot of offbeat things. I think he really needed the work, to be honest with you.'

Indeed, Robert knew that his underperforming films were hurting his reputation. Hollywood was a business and, as such, he needed a hit. And bad. Luckily, his next film would see him star with one of the world's biggest stars at the time. What could possibly go wrong?

7

COMEDOWN

'*It was not a particularly happy time creatively*'
ROBERT DOWNEY JR

Robert had decided that he needed to change his life. His first aim was to engineer a chance to star in a blockbuster – a sure thing that would bring him some box-office success. And teaming up with Mel Gibson on the war caper *Air America* looked about as sure a thing as you could get.

Robert had told his agent that he was desperate to work with Gibson and bizarrely enough the script for *Air America* landed on his lap. 'I did *Air America* for two reasons,' Robert said. 'To be in a movie with Mel Gibson and to make a bunch of money. And then underneath was the hope that in doing this formulaic thing I would be launched into a whole new realm of opportunity to do A-list movies. But by the time we were done, the only positive thing was meeting Mel Gibson.'

The two actors seemed an odd pairing. Robert came from a liberal background with an art-house sensibility, while Gibson was a strict Catholic with conservative values. But they would become very close and still have a bond to this day.

'When I first met him, I was detoxing from one of the seventy substances I'd been doing and my skin was a mess,' Robert recalled. 'When I met his family, one of his kids pointed at me and said to Mel, "He's got the measles!" We both laughed and I knew things between us were going to be OK.

'I think he kind of sees himself in me, what he was like before the first *Mad Max* came out. The brash, self-confident guy. He already had a family by then, so I guess I helped him to be a bit more of a guy, you know.'

Based on the 1979 book of the same name by Christopher Robbins, *Air America* was based on a true story of the Vietnam era. It centred on the CIA's covert activities in Laos, where US forces would help supply anti-communist forces with food and medical supplies, as well as drugs and guns. Kevin Costner, Bill Murray, Tom Cruise, Jim Belushi and Sean Connery had all been linked to the project before Robert and Gibson were hired. Robert was to play Billy Covington, the young pilot who finds himself enmeshed in all sorts of lunacy and corruption.

Robert wanted to take the role seriously. He had already attempted to sort out his drug problems several times, attending rehab programs from 1987. 'Even shame didn't work,' he said. 'I don't know what makes people change. Maybe you just get bored. It's like wanting to make your bed every morning, because you know you feel better if the bed is made when you come home. And then not coming home. So by the time you come home, the made bed reminds you only that you haven't been back for two days. I've beaten myself up about going back and forth between my dark and light sides so much. Probably that was the worst of all of it, what I did to myself by going straight past understanding into shame and self-denigration.

'Some part of me always felt like I would never amount to anything and there I was, starting to amount to something, at least on the outside. So what was going on and what my beliefs were about myself were not coinciding. I had a desire for buffers.

'This other part of me feels like there's been voices calling to me for a long time. Most of them are creative, real quiet things. But if you listen to those voices you also have to listen to the ones who whisper homicidal scenarios while you're in the shower. It's all the same voice.

'I've thought that my battles with my demons were over a million times and they just weren't. But the idea of passing on something that might go back to fucking Edwardian times in my family tree, of not stopping those patterns – no, no, we gotta rewrite that one. I don't want any excuses for failure any more, except one: I tried my best and it didn't work. I want to live a little more in the future now, have a dialogue with a hopeful future self. As opposed to reacting to clove-smoking, Miller Lite-chugging, Douglas-Park-throwing-up-in, sixteen-year-old girl-crazy high-school drop-out energy, which would be happy to talk to me still.

'What's amazing is, no matter how much I fuck up, it keeps straightening itself out. Walking the line between creativity and self-destruction scares me. People have always said to me, "The only thing that can stand in your way is you." But there's something so enticing about riding that fine line. And being alone scares me. I always seem to want to surround myself with people. I guess I love people and I also like night-lights.'

At the beginning of the shoot, Robert attempted to get into the character's head but quickly realised that the film was less internal than more about harnessing the energy between him and Gibson. 'This time I went out and did all this research,' he said. 'Billy was from San Diego and he was a Navy brat. Maybe because this film was an action movie, I didn't use any of it. None of it mattered and none of it worked.

'He is a pilot, a free spirit – for once I play the guy who isn't the weirdest guy around. He's not a *normal*

King of the world – *Iron Man* removed any doubt that Robert Downey
Jr was a star without rival.

© *Rex Features*

Left: Downey with his mother Elise in 2009.

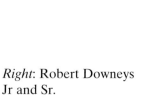

Right: Robert Downeys Jr and Sr.

A 1986 sketch on *Saturday Night Live* with Downey. © *Rex Features*

Above: Downey with actor Michael Anthony Hall, rocker David Lee Roth and actor Sonia Braga.

© *Getty Images*

Below: *Tuff Turf* from 1985 with Downey, far right, leaning on James Spader.

© *Rex Features*

Above: Another mid-80s teen smash – Downey with Hall, Ilan Mitchell Smith and Robert Rusler cooking up some *Weird Science*.   © *Rex Features*

Below: Mel Gibson and Downey take to the *Air America* in 1990.

© *Rex Features*

Right: Downey in *Soapdish* from 1991. *© Rex Features*

Below: A still from *Chaplin*. *© Rex Features*

Above: Richard
Attenborough directed
Downey as Chaplin in the
biopic of the comedian.
© *Rex Features*

Left: Downey in character.
© *Rex Features*

Left: On the set of 1994's
Restoration with wife
Deborah Falconer.

© *Rex Features*

Right: Downey won a
Golden Globe for Best
Supporting Actor in a
TV Series in 2001. *Ally
McBeal* starred, right,
Calista Flockhart.

© *Rex Features*

guy, really, but he starts realising that he's about as sane as they come in this world he enters. This was physically the riskiest film I've ever done but not the toughest – jumping out of planes wasn't scary. Trying to get in touch with the higher aspects of yourself is.'

The hugely complicated production would see the film being shot in several locations, including Thailand, London and Los Angeles. Twenty-six aircraft, five hundred crewmembers and more than a dozen cameras would be used in a shoot that would be disrupted by earthquakes and typhoons.

In Thailand, Robert and crewmembers would cause mischief with fireworks. 'See, the Thais are great. They do really crazy stuff, but then it's over. It's like, three days of craziness, then no more. But we're Americans. We were like, "It ain't over till it's over." The guy who ran the hotel we stayed at would cringe and say, "Oh, they're at it again."

'There were all the darker aspects of our country in Thailand. Only it's not hidden. Drugs, prostitution, crime, oppression – it's like in the entertainment guide. There's still that aspect of wholesale destruction of the sanctity of femaleness and all that, and then you go up in the mountains and there's the monks in their robes and you can feel like you've never been in a more blissful, loving place in your life.

'I went with Mel Gibson for a holiday in Bangkok. I had planned to spend a weekend there, but after twenty-four hours I went running back to the movie set in the jungle. Bangkok was so depressing. People would come running up offering their eight-year-old sister, who they insisted was a virgin. Any sexual perversion you wanted you could find if you were willing to pay for it. I was so grossed out, I said goodbye to Mel and went right back to the set. I think a little bit of me died – it was like a nightmare. If there's a hell, then it's probably called Bangkok.

'But we're on location and I just remember like, just what a dog means there. It's a little different. There was some puppy running around the set one minute and then I just looked out my trailer door and this truck just backed up over it and just, ugh, slushed it. I didn't expect to see that kind of disregard for something that we, as Americans, would be like, "Not the puppy!" It's really weird to think that other places, or maybe other aspects of what we consider to be our American way, are just callous and that kind of fucked up.'

It's clear that during the shoot Robert attempted to clean himself up, turning down drinks and getting up early in the morning to go jogging. He was certainly talking a good game, stating in interviews, 'This is the 1990s. That whole scene is over and I'm really glad I'm not over too. I was at a party the other night where I saw a whole bunch of people on coke and it was scary.

'It's dangerous. Drinking is dangerous. Drinking and driving is crazy. I have too much stuff to do to mess with dangerous chemicals. There is alcoholism in this country. There is drug dependency in this country. And I don't know anyone who hasn't lost someone to alcoholism or drugs.'

But the making of *Air America* and its subsequent poor takings at the box office would leave him disappointed, if not entirely surprised. It became quickly clear that the film was a tired attempt at a buddy movie. The glint in both of the leading men's eyes weren't apparent in the film. 'I'm not going to be doing a big action movie for a long time,' Robert would add. 'Unless it's something that really has something to say. No one gets killed gratuitously in this film – it's not like one of those bang, bang, bang bullshit things – but it's just so tedious! It's acting, but the acting comes from just bearing it, getting through all the technical shit as opposed to interacting with someone, taking some chances, making some huge mistake.

'You feel you have to do the commercial films in order to keep your visibility high and your agents and managers happy, but you want to do films that are important, too. That's pretty much the same way I've been running my career. But since *Air America*, which was one for them, I've decided that's bullshit. From now on, it's all for me.'

A disenchanted Robert would later dub the movie *Air Generica* and move on – 'Regardless of the final product, I got the money and I worked with Mel' – but at least he and his father were now enjoying a much healthier relationship. 'I've start realising how we're a lot more alike,' Robert said.

Robert Downey Sr had remarried and was living with writer Laura Ernst only two blocks from Robert in LA. Talking about the two men's similarities, Laura said, 'They don't really have to say much to each other and I can see in Jr's work that he has learned a lot from his father. They have similar styles. Jr is up for trying anything. He's very interesting to watch. Absolutely doesn't edit himself ever. That's remarkable to watch.'

The first step in Robert's change of direction was to team with his dad for 1990's *Too Much Sun*, a comedy about a multimillionaire's inheritance.

Downey Sr recalled, 'Somebody gave me a script at a race track and said "Bob, what do you think?" I read it and I said, "There's a germ here but I think I can get it done. It was really one man and his son and he's dying, and he tells his son, "You're not getting a dime until you give me a child," and he's not interested in women. So boring, but there was something to that. So Laura and I put in the ladies and the priest. The studio said, "Give me a couple of names and we can do it."

Downey Sr found out that his son had cache with the studio and it must have given Robert some satisfaction that his name helped secure finance for his dad's film. 'That movie wouldn't have gotten out without him. That's reality,' said Downey Sr.

Talking about his son, he said, 'The first night he shows up he's come from *Air America* and he's happy to be with us. The first night [actress] Andrea Martin is singing and he starts masturbating under the covers. The crew is at pains laughing. We were keeling over. He doesn't even crack a smile. I'm like, "That's funny to me." He goes, "Good, hope you can use it." That was the first night and it went uphill from there. He's fun to have around.

'*Too Much Sun* isn't the greatest screenplay,' he added. 'But we had fun. It was fun to make it, but it's not one I'll see over and over. But I liked it.'

'Pretty good,' was Robert's verdict. 'It's funny. It's about a gay brother and lesbian sister – Eric Idle and Andrea Martin – whose father is dying and says he going to leave his money to whoever has a kid first. It doesn't deal with homosexuality responsibly, but it's not supposed to. That makes me a little uneasy, but I know that my father is so accepting it's not like he's not aware. He's extremely talented.'

Next Robert would star in the romantic comedy *Soapdish*. Describing his character, Downey said he was 'a young prick producer in Armani suits. I want to take a modern-day Mephistopheles kind of angle on it. I want to make him more likeable than I am, which is pretty hefty. I make the mistake of stepping down to characters as opposed to shooting up. It's an ego thing to think, "This character is a little faction of me, a little of that, but not endowed with any of the things that make me *me*." This time, I want to make people uncomfortable liking this guy, knowing that, underneath, he really is still an asshole.

'I've just gotta show up. It would be really nice to be in a great film, but it's not time yet. If I ever wind up being in a great film, it'll mean so much more to me now. But I know this: I'm going to get much better.'

He wasn't wrong. *Soapdish* would be another film where he would just 'phone in' his performance. 'It was still better than anyone else,' he added. 'But it felt like a scam, like shoplifting. Every film coming out was like snapping another sensor off a sweater, draping it around my waist and chatting with the security guards as I walked out.'

Career-wise, Robert was depressed. It just wasn't happening for him. He tried to play the studio game and he got burned. He wanted to entertain his audience, find a script that would speak out to him, but there was nothing that excited him. Then his personal life took a turn for the worse when he and Sarah Jessica Parker separated. He had believed that they 'weren't beyond reconciliation' when it happened – but 'then I read in the papers that she's gallivanting with one of the Kennedy boys.

'We had real deep love for each other and I worshipped her. When I could. I don't know that I would have had a career at all without her. She gave me something more than work. Sarah helped me get clean. She was there for me every step of the way. I think she saved my life. No, I know she saved my life.

He added, 'The running joke, particularly when I was with Sarah Jessica – she would say, "You just made more money in your last six weeks than I've made in my whole career, and yet I have money and you're broke and asking me for five grand. What are you doing?" I'd say, "I don't know. I'll check the trunk I'm sure there's a bag of something or other that will explain it."

'I liked to drink and I had a drug problem and that didn't jibe with Sarah Jessica, because it is the furthest thing from what she is. She provided me a home and understanding. She tried to help me. She was so miffed when I didn't get my act together.'

For her part, she said in a 1996 interview, 'He's one of those tortured souls. I'd never seen cocaine in my life and my boyfriend was addicted to it. Having no experience in that world of drugs and having very little understanding of why you just can't give it up if you know it's so destructive, I just found it incredibly difficult to deal with. You start out worried and understanding and sympathetic, and then you turn angry and bitter and resentful and not particularly loving. It's terrible. You feel so impotent. You're always wondering and waiting for a call from someone saying, "We went to his trailer to get him and he's dead." I felt so sad and, by the end, I felt exhausted.

'Everyone who knew us said this would never last. We were seemingly completely different personalities: he was such an extrovert while I was an introvert. He helped me a lot in going out, being courageous, not wanting to throw up all night. He was probably the most eccentric person I'd ever met, very mercurial and odd but also completely open, emotionally right there.'

'I was dishonest with her a lot,' Robert admitted. 'I think after a certain point you break a trust with someone and you can't repair it any more. Also, she was growing and learning and really becoming a woman. I looked to her for security and at the same time didn't level with her about a lot of stuff. You name it – other women, too much partying.

'Parker liked things like watching CNN and staying involved in events, having dinner parties with friends and reading novels. That was great for me, because I had a safe place. But I was pulling 360s in the Universal parking lot and disappearing for three days for things one needs blood transfusions to recuperate from.'

Distraught, Robert attempted to start a new phase in his life, by getting his house blessed. 'A beautiful four-hundred-pound black woman named Marsala went through the house and sang. I wanted to clear out that old energy, because I'd lived there with Sarah Jessica Parker for five years almost... It's a Native American ritual using sage to clear the energy out of whatever area you're in.'

Not that Robert moped around for long. In May

1992 he would marry actress Deborah Falconer, who he had only dated for a month or so before marrying her. They had met four years earlier but she was in another relationship. However, after meeting at a show their relationship quickly blossomed. 'It was really her personality,' he said, 'though it was of great benefit that she happens to be one of the most drop-dead gorgeous women I'd ever seen. There's something really youthful about her. She isn't self-conscious about how beautiful she is. And I could not get over her ass.'

As ever with Robert, things didn't go as planned. Their first date was interrupted by his family and friends, trying to stage an intervention for him. They felt his life was getting out of control. She said, 'They were all looking at me like I was the Devil's child. Like, "Pack up your stuff, honey – you'll never see him again."' But the couple would eventually marry at Deborah's mother's backyard in California.

'Not to slight Sarah in the slightest, it seemed eventually Sarah and I would have married,' Robert said. 'But once certain words are said, or once you separated yourself geographically from a relationship, it's a whole different game. It's like pulling the one-armed bandit. And I came up gold bars a lot quicker than expected.

'My wife Deborah started working quite a bit as an actress right about the time we first met. She was starting to get big parts, but one morning she just said to me, "You know what? I don't want to do this any more." I said, "Why?" and she said, "Because I don't like it. I don't like getting up at seven in the morning. I don't like having to be made an object of people's desire that I don't know. I just want to be with you." I swear to God, it just changed my life. I was like, "I can't believe you're saying this. I love you.'"

8

DOWNEY GOES SILENT AND CAUSES A BIG NOISE

'Chaplin has been an undercurrent my whole life'
ROBERT DOWNEY JR

Robert had always been a huge Charlie Chaplin fan. He had bought a house in LA that Chaplin had lived in, and he used to re-enact some of the silent actor's favourite sketches with his friends. And in 1991 he tried on Chaplin's shoes at the Museum of the Moving Image in London. ('They fit perfectly, we have the same feet.') So, when Robert learned that Sir Richard Attenborough was making a biopic of the movie great, Robert knew it had to be him.

Knowing that the director was in the same office as his agent, he met him with the words, 'I am the one actor, Mr Attenborough, to play Charlie Chaplin. One day you'll come back to me. Goodbye, I'm very glad to have met you.'

However, Attenborough wasn't convinced. 'I first met Robert in my agent's office in Los Angeles,' he said. 'There was a knock on the door and this young man came in with hair sticking out in spikes with big black boots and rings in his ears – I'm not even sure he didn't have a ring in his nose. He was absolutely LA Brat Pack, there was no question of that whatsoever. All he did was announce that he was going to play Chaplin, that he was the one actor who could play Chaplin and would I test him? I agreed. I can't say that I was totally convinced at that point. Obviously I would have preferred an English actor to have played a character who was born and bred in the East End of London, as Charlie was, but I couldn't find one.'

Like Robert, Attenborough had been smitten by Chaplin and was desperate to make a biopic. But first he needed permission. 'A marvellous thing happened when I first wrote to Oona (Charlie's fourth wife). Charlie had died and I wrote to Oona some three and a half years ago to ask for her agreement to make this movie. Because, obviously we needed the rights to Charlie's autobiography [and] we needed the rights to David [Robinson]'s book.

'Oona said, "You may make the film, as you wish to make it. You may have all the documents. You may have all the archives. You may have anything that any of the family can give you. We only have one condition. We don't wish to have any approvals whatsoever, whether on the script, or the casting, or anything to do with the movie. That is your decision."

'It's not a sycophantic piece of work,' the director insisted. 'Nothing has been hidden from us. We show his predilection for girls in their teens. We show his absolutely blinkered life in terms of his work, which took precedence over everything. We show his ruthlessness. We show all the tough sides of this man.'

While Robert was convinced he could play the part, many, many other actors felt they were equally right for it. Billy Crystal, Robin Williams and a young Jim Carrey were just some of the big names considered. As Attenborough stated, casting the actor was going to be hard.

'There are obviously, as far as Charlie is concerned, a number of prerequisites that are absolutely essential. In the first place, Charlie went to America when he was nineteen, was making his own movies at the age of twenty-five, and by the time he was thirty he was a millionaire and probably the most famous man in the world. You have to have somebody who can play those ages. Because although the picture begins at the age of five, the leading actor has to begin at the age of eighteen or nineteen and has to go to the age of eighty-three. You also have the problem of height. Charlie was not very tall and, whereas you can turn Alan Ladd into Duke Wayne, you can't turn Duke Wayne into Alan Ladd and so we had to have an actor who was somewhere around five foot six and a half, five seven, something like that.

'Now making Charlie look like The Tramp was relatively easy, but making somebody look like Charlie as he was off the screen is very much more difficult. So you've got to achieve that. You've also got to have somebody who's immensely agile.

'Another requirement was to find an actor with Charlie's amazing agility who could not only pull off the stunts Charlie used to do, but could also replicate his distinctive stance. If you ever saw Chaplin out of character he walked and stood very much like a marionette. Finally, we needed an actor who had a fine ear for accents. Anyone can walk along twiddling a cane but it takes a man of real talent to capture Charlie's changing Cockney accent, which had a peculiarly pedantic edge to it.

'You also, of course, have somebody who is a sensational actor and I would refer everybody merely to the great Olivier, who said that he believed that Chaplin was the greatest actor of all time. Now if you put all those things together, and you also need a tremendous charisma and an immense acting ability, you are constrained obviously. I considered over the three years or so, every major English and American actor that could possibly play the part.'

However, Robert continued to pester the director about the part. 'I met him a couple more times and he asked me to screen test,' recalls Downey. 'I really worked my butt off for the screen test. I got a dialect coach and an acting coach.

'He asked me to come into this room with a ladder and be funny in the tramp outfit. So I did – or I tried. I got my foot stuck in the door and kind of did some business. After that, they put some gray in my hair and a 1930s suit on and had me improvise, asking me where Charlie had been that day. Luckily, I'd been reading enough of the autobiography.

As Attenborough recalled, 'We had interviews and long sessions with between twenty-five and thirty [actors]. We tested seven. Full tests. Full make-up tests, full acting tests and everything else. There was, in my opinion, no doubt whatsoever that, at the end of the day, one person was head and shoulders above everybody else, not merely in fulfilling the requirements, but in talent... To convey a genius of the complexity of Chaplin is a very great task, but what was remarkable was that he provided the fire in the belly and turmoil behind the eyes.

'This was vital because, of all the words that should be selected as far as Charlie is concerned, the key one is the word "passion". He was passionate about everything that he did, whether it was his love affairs or whether it was his commitment to what he thought was the right way to behave in terms of the subject matter that he chose or whether it was the overriding passion of his work. Passion controlled everything. Once you accept that, a mass of other things falls into place and that's what Robert had. Robert had the ability to convey that driving, unqualified determination to achieve what he set out to achieve.

Robert said, 'This is why I'll really be indebted to [Attenborough] on certain levels forever. He would not waver from his decision on me playing the part... And everyone took a pay cut to do this movie. I mean, everyone. Richard took the biggest. I got paid more for doing *Soapdish* and not being in the whole movie and just wearing a bunch of suits and cracking jokes.'

Typically, it wouldn't be as easy as Robert getting the part of his life: there was a huge scare that the film might not happen. With Attenborough finding his star, he thought the film was a go-ahead – until Universal decided to pull the plug on the project.

Attenborough said, 'There would be delays to the film getting made. I have to admit that the answer is a little complicated in that I had a contractual commitment with Universal, then Universal for various reasons pulled out of the picture. And we went to [the production company] Carolco and I don't think Carolco was able to raise funds in the UK.

'The picture folded on a Friday afternoon, which I shall never forget, with Universal. And I had known for a number of years that [producer] Mario Kassar had always been an enormous fan of the idea of a picture about Charlie. And was a great authority on him. And so when it fell, my agent in Los Angeles said the person to talk to at once was Mario Kassar. On the Sunday we spent the morning with Mario and Mario said, "I'll make it." So then we had to await rescheduling, rebudgeting with all the delays and so on.

'I really do not know [why Universal pulled out]. Genuinely, I don't know whether it was the budget. I really have no idea, other than I can say they put the picture "in turnaround" quite suddenly.'

For his part, Robert would say, 'Even if this movie had never gone ahead, knowing that if it had been done it would have been done with me would have been reward enough.' However, the movie now had the go-ahead and Robert would throw himself into research for the role.

'Ultimately, there is no way I will ever be able to approach the expertise [Chaplin] had with things,' Robert said. 'He was completely God-gifted and he had the experience of twenty years of burlesque and fifty years of filmmaking. But there's a lot of stuff in this movie about him as a man – his relations with the succession of great beauties who passed through his life and with his children. And the political stuff that led to his exile from America in the 1950s for being a left-winger. That sort of thing makes up most of the movie and I'm just immersing myself in the material. I wonder how English people will feel about me playing Chaplin. Being an American, I have a feeling a lot of people will want to nail me for it. But I do have the advantage of being short. And as for the American aspect, he did come here early and spent the major portion of his career here.

It was a part that would devour Robert – and one that would finally see him mature as an actor. 'I started off basically watching a lot of the films and then read everything to some of the most obscure material you could find. I think for me that the most difficult thing has been dealing with what I feel the responsibility is. I think when you have someone who was an entertainer, but also so much a social concave – I just hope that Charlie would feel that I've done some service to the part and that's something I can only hope for.'

Attenborough confirmed Robert's passion for the role. 'He spent months before we started working and every single day follows that through in relation to his accent and his cockney accent. Charlie had a broad, broad, broad cockney accent and maintained it for really quite a long time in his life and only later refined it. And that accent of course is another of the prerequisites, or rather the capability of the actor, to be able to portray that character with the accent. Robert's cockney accent is impeccable in the movie. And impeccable because he is an extraordinary mimic and secondly because he has worked as hard as any actor that I have dealt with in those terms.'

Robert had two dialect coaches – one to perfect the cockney accent, the other for the upper-class dialect – plus two coaches for movement. There was even a coach to teach him how to play tennis left-handed. 'I didn't have to,' Robert said, 'but it was an opportunity to really go for broke and nail the character as much as I could. I know the production side often thought, "The heck with it." You know, when the sun was going down and I was still serving them over to Beirut.'

He was also granted full access to the Chaplin archives at the Museum of the Moving Image in London. 'They let me try on his *Great Dictator* outfit, as well as his shoes. It was like being backstage in Charlie Chaplin's world. Then, a week before we started shooting, I tried on his *City Lights* jacket. Being an American, I checked the pockets and found a cigar stub – probably left over from the scene where the millionaire has kicked him out and he gets a cigar off the street. I don't know, I guess the British never thought to check the pockets.

'When I was doing Chaplin I remember I created this wall and by the time I was done I was calling David Robinson, who wrote the definitive biography of Chaplin, telling him there was a typo on page seventy-nine and he was like, "My dear, have some tea." I've gone pretty nuts, but it's because I care.

'I got some pretty obscure material, too – some of those real dusty ones in the back of the freak shops. Of course, I watched all the movies as much as I could and employed some interesting techno stuff as well, like printing out digital images of certain Chaplin expressions. There were so many subtleties. His bag of tricks was so immense from years and years of training on the London stage with the vaudeville acts.'

However, Robert's research began to leave him with bouts of depression. Wildly competitive, he thought that he couldn't be as gifted and imaginative as Chaplin, and this gnawed at him. That was when Attenborough's experience came in handy. He just knew that Robert needed confidence and comfort. And lots of it. During shooting, it was clear that, while Robert was an incredibly gifted talent, he was still very raw. Guided by Attenborough's steady hands, Robert would finally show everyone what he was fully capable of.

'Sir Richard was brilliant,' remembered Robert. 'He couldn't have been more helpful. I was like a pregnant woman going through a particularly difficult labour and Sir Richard was the dedicated midwife. I felt he would never ask me to do things he couldn't help me through – he would go through every moment with me. I would ring him up in the middle of the night because I couldn't sleep for worrying about some small detail of Charlie's life and he never seemed to mind. He might suggest that it could wait until morning but he never minded being called.

'He also had the knack of helping me in exactly the way that I wanted. There's a scene in the movie in which Charlie watches footage of the Great War. It must have been an incredibly distressing experience for him because he was watching his fellow countrymen die in the trenches at a time when he was feeling guilty about making movies in Hollywood. All I knew about war was seeing American newsreels from Vietnam, yet Sir Richard was able to talk me through this and let me know exactly the way Chaplin would have felt at seeing this devastating footage.

'I feel my performances in this film had a lot to do with a lot of other people but primarily with Sir Richard. There were a lot of things that I simply didn't know before we started and I think I'm a very different person from the one I was before, and part of that has to do with our relationship. When someone who has been making films twice as long as I've been sucking air takes time to really give me so much of his experience and knowledge, that's really important. He never changed his mind when the studio lacked faith in me. He really was my champion and I was prepared to do whatever I had to do for him.'

Moira Kelly played Chaplin's fourth wife, Oona O'Neill. 'Moira and Robert worked marvellously together,' said the director. 'I didn't even test Moira. I didn't look at any of the movies. I just knew.'

Robert added, 'The first day we shot her dailies, it was like watching Elizabeth Taylor's screen test. We were like, "Oh, that's what they mean about presence." There's something about Moira that kind of woke up a part of me. The whole film was that way.'

She said about Robert in return, 'He talks in fables.

He reminds me of the caterpillar in *Alice in Wonderland*. Everything's a riddle. He's an ever-changing thing, like a chameleon. He'll try to be responsible. But that doesn't mean he can't still be creative or playful or destructive. I don't think he had a childhood. I suppose that's why he's such a boy now.'

Attenborough also cast Charlie's real-life daughter, Geraldine, as her own grandmother, Hannah. 'My father talked about Hannah a lot and with great affection,' she said. 'He adored her. He never said she was insane but he would tell funny stories about her and we could see that she was. I was always tempted to be in the film, though, because it was going to be a major motion picture with Sir Richard directing and it was such a wonderful part. I didn't realise, though, that it would be so painful until I saw Hannah on the screen. It was a great part, but a real blow to see her like that.'

Attenborough would show Geraldine some footage that had already been shot of Robert playing her father. She said, 'I have to tell you: I had never, ever dreamed that anybody could convince me that they were Daddy. But that young man *was* Daddy. I don't think that any actor could do what Robert did. It was as if my father came down from Heaven and inhabited him and possessed him for the length of the movie. It was just so shocking – he's extraordinary. It's as if my father was there, or else Robert in his reincarnation.

'He is so gorgeous, which is appropriate because

my father was a beautiful man too. Robert does the Little Tramp perfectly and he seems to capture the essence of my father. He's heartbreaking and he has my father's sense of melancholy. The first time I met him as the Little Tramp I hugged him and he hugged me, and there I was with my father as a young man in my arms. We had quite a Freudian moment there.'

Exhausted and drained he might have been, but Robert felt hugely proud of his performance in the film. Attenborough had wrung every bit of effort out of his leading man and it was all there up on screen. His dad said, 'You didn't drop the ball once.'

'That's the first time he said that,' remarked Robert.

The *New York Times* also noted, 'Robert Downey Jr ... is good and persuasive as the adult Charlie when the material allows and close to brilliant when he does some of Charlie's early vaudeville and film sketches. His slapstick routines are graceful, witty and, most important, really funny.'

Robert was nominated for an Oscar for his performance and he has gone on record claiming that he thought he 'totally deserved to win'. However, when Al Pacino's name was called out for his performance in *Scent of a Woman*, Robert recalled, 'The guy who had the camera on me as I smiled and got up and gave the ovation to Pacino said, "Now that was discipline." I thought for a second I was going to win. Marisa Tomei had won and I thought, "It's the young people here." I'm sitting there, convinced this could be it. The voiceover in my head was just ridiculous. It's all going my way. Not much longer now. Why is it the last category? Because it's *the* category. Richard Tyler designed this suit for me. I'm going to go up and show it off. I kind of look like Daniel Day-Lewis. He won last time. It's all coming together. Then it's, "Hey, Robert, you want to go to the after-party?" Oh, yeah. Good. That was just fucked.'

While Robert was widely praised for his performance in the film and rightly so, the movie itself was somewhat panned by critics. Most believed that by trying to cover all of Chaplin's life it was spread too thin. It was an opinion that Robert now shares, saying, 'It could have been the next *Citizen Kane*. It wasn't Attenborough's fault. We simply forgot to make a great movie.'

Attenborough went on to say that, if Robert chose his roles right, he would go on to be a huge star.

'I will never do another *Chances Are* or *Air America* again,' Robert said. 'I'd sell my house before I made a movie that didn't feel right. Part of me feels that acting is my job – a damn good living and I don't want to give up the lifestyle – but another part is just starting to recognise the tertiary, healing element to art. I have to believe that there's something, some greater purpose, for my doing it, because, really, nobody has any business playing Charlie Chaplin.'

9

LIFE AFTER CHAPLIN

*'If you want your film to have a lousy opening
weekend just throw me in it, because I've never
been in a film that was a big hit'*
ROBERT DOWNEY JR

Chaplin changed life for Robert Downey Jr.
After Attenborough's vote of confidence he was
sure he was going to capitalise on the acclaim that he
received. First up was the 1993 supernatural comedy
Heart and Souls. 'It's kind of a spiritual comedy,'
Robert said. 'I play a guy who goes and shuts down
companies and enjoys it, but by the end of the movie
decides to change. Anyway, it's nice and fun. And I
don't have to be in make-up.'

Life was good for Robert. 'San Francisco, lots
of money, Deb was pregnant. Probably one of the
best times in my life. Good movie,' was how he
remembered that time.

His son Indio was born on 7 September 1993, and his friend Michael Anthony Hall was the baby's godfather. Talking about becoming a parent, Robert added, 'It was the first time I recognised that there was something a lot more difficult than working. A lot more rewarding. Suddenly, your primary focus is outside yourself.

'It's so much more important to me what Indio's watching on TV in the trailer than what I'm doing on the set,' he added. 'I find myself obsessing about things like his dental hygiene.

'It's amazing how many things can happen once and scar a kid so I'm proud of the way we've been with our son. I love the times I'm not working. I love the routine of taking my kid to breakfast at this coffee shop he likes. At home, I'm big on the Discovery Channel and the Learning Channel. I think you can just sit there and grow smart.'

When asked about her ex-boyfriend being a father, Sarah Jessica Parker said, 'Five or six years ago, we didn't discuss being parents. It didn't matter what I wanted. It was clear that, accidental or not, parenthood was something you would impose on Downey. He always wanted to be a grown-up and I think he's pursuing it – although not successfully. Now he's trying to be selfless. After Indio was born, he said to me – and I couldn't believe it because it was so cliché – "Wow, I'm not the centre of attention any more."'

Downey Sr added, 'Having a son changed Robert

big time. It made him see that the world has some kind of order to it. It's about... It's about... That's exactly the word – boundaries. Teach your children boundaries, how to recognise and set your own. As a father, I'm very protective, which is weird. Think about the way a lot of guys drive. You're on a hill and you pass somebody going seventy when you should be doing forty-five. I'd never, ever, dream of doing anything but the speed limit with Indio in the car. It's a great excuse for me to become that hidden grandpa I am all the time anyway.'

Robert would add, 'Could you imagine if I was your dad? Think about it. It sounds hypocritical, doesn't it? I think boundaries are good when raising children and the other thing I am obsessed about lately is honesty.'

Screenwriter-director James Toback (who had worked with Robert on *The Pick-Up Artist*) added, 'The relationship I saw with him and Indio is as good a father–son relationship as any I've ever seen. I mean, they have a great rapport and he treats his son with respect.

A diversion from his usual career path saw Robert work on the revealing documentary *The Last Party*, in which he looked at the political conventions of the 1992 US electoral campaign. 'I was twenty-seven years old and I didn't know what a delegate was,' he said frankly. 'I saw it as an opportunity to learn about myself and this country.'

The film's co-director, Marc Levin, said, 'We picked a pop star [Robert] who admitted he didn't know much about the system. But he's a part of the same orbit. That's how this whole thing works now – it's like a movie.'

Producer Josh Richman added, 'Originally we were just going to do it about the Democratic convention. But we needed money, so I asked Robert and suddenly we were making a feature film [about the Republican convention as well].

The film sees Robert appear with his dad, who would say, 'He doesn't know much about politics so it was cute.'

Robert would add, 'I want to learn the pros and cons of the issues, but ultimately I have to ask what feels right inside of me and ultimately that's all there is for everybody. And I know that that's going to be up for scrutiny but, in my perception, the people that will scrutinise that are people who have long lost touch, at least seemingly, with those deep-rooted feelings or emotions of what feels right.

'I was such a – not that I'm not now – but I was a total ignoramus about not even politics, but anything that had to do with anything else except my own selfish interests. I just thought it would be a really cool opportunity. I leaned a lot and at the same time, in the aftermath, I realised I was all fuckin' gung-ho about Clinton. There was that bias in the documentary. I was just jumping on the bandwagon.

That's what I learned the most from it – a year later watching it. Everybody has unconscious biases about everything. Everybody about everything.

Later he would say, 'Never need to go to another convention. Thank God,' and, 'It was exhausting and pointless.'.

1993 also saw Robert appear in a small role in Robert Altman's excellent *Short Cuts*, followed by a supporting role as Wayne Gale in Oliver Stone's controversial *Natural Born Killers*.

The latter movie was based on a screenplay by *Pulp Fiction*'s Quentin Tarantino, but his work is hardly evident after Oliver Stone rewrote the script to such an extent that Tarantino was given a story credit only. 'It's not going to be my movie,' said Tarantino. 'It's going to be Oliver Stone's and God bless him. I hope he does a good job with it. If I wasn't emotionally attached to it, I'm sure I would find it very interesting. If you like my stuff, you might not like this movie. But if you like his stuff, you're probably going to love it. It might be the best thing he's ever done, but not because of anything to do with me. I actually can't wait to see it, to tell you the truth.'

The story of a couple who go on a killing spree interested Stone, but he felt the movie needed to be focused more on how the media would react to such a situation following the Rodney King incident and the OJ Simpson murder trial. 'When I started this was a surreal piece,' Stone told *Time* magazine. 'Now, thanks to Bobbitt and Menendez and Tonya Harding, it's become satire. By the time I'd finished, fact had caught up to fiction. OJ is the final blow-out.'

To get into the role of a newscaster, Robert spent time with the notorious Australian TV shock king and *New York Post* columnist Steve Dunleavy.

'I love *Natural Born Killers* a whole bunch,' Robert said in 2006. 'I followed Steve Dunleavy around to research the role and the one dominating thing I got from him was his relentlessness. It's like he's running a race every day. It never stops.

'I actually had a lot of fun with him and, at the end of the day, I'd still have thirty or forty minutes of good material left in me. I'd walk in a restaurant and start acting like him. When people heard that Australian accent booming across the room, they knew some funny stuff was going to happen. And I'd be happy to oblige them.'

Robert had actually wanted to use an English accent, but Stone thought it was too soon following *Chaplin*.

'I'll be surprised if I wind up doing a film that is as violent as that again,' Robert continued, 'just because I think of the energy that you get into with it and the mindset that you get into. If it's possible for me to get through the rest of my career, however long that is, without having to do anything that gives people stomach-aches, that would be nice.

'I had never been in a situation where there was

more than enough money to do whatever the director wanted. It was very experimental in lots of ways and it was just really fun. I remember that period of time when it was so safe and fun to be out of your gourd then go work really hard and do a real trippy, cool movie.

'We shot a big part of the film in a real prison and that was tough. Oliver likes to stretch his crew's efforts to the limit and those who are not used to his working methods sometimes have a hard time adapting. But that was an incredible experience.

'Oliver Stone kept playing loud industrial music all the time on the set. The only respite would be towards the end of the day when he'd put some Leonard Cohen on. The rest of the time, it was pandemonium. I'm talking about music that was so loud you couldn't hear the special effects guy telling you how many blank rounds were chambered in your Glock.'

He would add of his own situation, 'I've been pretty focused for the last couple of years and I've also been fortunate working with good directors. I think if you work with directors of that calibre, you wind up having a better likelihood of being nominated for an Academy Award. I just don't like setting myself up to be disappointed, so I'll just say, "Yeah, that would be great." It's out of my hands.'

Defending the film in the subsequent controversy over its violence, Stone said, 'Let's look at the statistics. Violent crime has remained flat over the past twenty years. But the perception of crime has changed; now it's the "Number One" enemy. Every night on the news it's back-to-back murder and body bags. Even the national news is perverted, because the news has become a profit-oriented enterprise. It's the old yellow journalism. Now that communism is dead, they need new demons. This virus has infected us all – the demons within us and among us.'

Next Robert would also star in Norman Jewison's romantic comedy *Only You*. 'I was laughing out loud when I was reading it,' Robert said. 'How great to be able to be paid to do the kind of film that you like to watch.' When it came to filming, however, Robert struggled at first because 'the *Natural Born Killers* character was still with me'.

'Robert has always had charm,' said Jewison, 'but he never used it in the way other actors have used their charm. All of his roles demand so much and he is always in character and interesting to watch, but he's never been allowed to play a kind of starring role – with style and charm – until this film. He's like Tony Curtis: charming with great comedic timing ... in the way he just seduces the audience.'

Only You proved to be Robert's biggest pay day yet – he picked up $2.2million for six weeks' work.

His next role was in the 1995 comedy-drama *Home for Holidays* – a film he would remember for all the wrong reasons.

The screenplay for *Home for the Holidays* arrived

on Jodie Foster's desk from her business partner, Stuart Kleinman, with a note saying, 'It's a complete mess. And I love it.'

'It was a mess and I fell in love with it too,' Foster said. 'The great challenge was to find a beautiful idea to pull through it, a narrative line that would make the story work and bring all the parts into the proper relationship.'

The script, by veteran screenwriter WD Richter, would end up being fine-tuned by the writer and Foster, and would tell the story of a thirty-something single woman who is having the Thanksgiving from Hell.

'I think what I responded to in the script is the universal phenomenon of the artificiality of the day,' Foster said. 'You step out of your normal life and you are asked to make a vow of love to people you don't really know and who don't really understand you. You wonder, "How can I love someone who doesn't get me?" It's like being stuck in an elevator with a bunch of strangers. And it all comes to loggerheads on this one day.'

Robert agreed to star in the drama as the central character's mischievous gay brother. Foster knew he was a great actor, but what she couldn't have known was that he was going though a dark period in his life.

'When I first got turned on to hard drugs as a teenager, I could snort coke and drink all night and still function,' Robert said. 'As soon as I started smoking heroin instead of smoking coke, everything was different and I knew it was. And it happened around the time I was doing *Home for the Holidays*.

'*Home for the Holidays* is, for me, one of the most relaxed performances in the history of cinema. I can't attribute that to the fact that I was at a serene place in my life, or that there was a real warm feeling on the set. I can't say that it wasn't real dark, real evil and real hurtful to those around me. And yet, practically every take of that film was a print.'

Foster quickly realised that Robert was out of control, handing him a handwritten note that read, 'Listen, I'm not worried about you on this film. You're not losing it or nodding out and you're giving a great performance. I'm worried about your thinking you can get away with doing this on another film.'

'Nonetheless, the experience was a ball.' Robert would say. 'My body felt great. I wasn't hungry. There are certain practical things that doing lots of heroin and cocaine takes care of. Like weight problems, or attention-deficit disorder. I could actually be interested in what someone was saying, when I wouldn't have been interested sober. Mostly I'm surprised that it didn't happen sooner. I mean, it's like running red lights all the time and finally getting a ticket.

'I'm very proud of that film. It's the rest of the day I cringe about.'

Robert's next movie was the period drama

Restoration, in which he played a physician who saves the life of someone close to King Charles II. The movie would see him teaming up once more with *Soapdish* director Michael Hoffman.

'I've certainly come to care a lot about Robert and have an immense respect and admiration for his talent,' the director said. 'His commitment on *Restoration* was really, really extraordinary. He is a remarkably inventive actor and although his performance in this movie is as good as you've ever seen him – really wonderful, simple and truthful – I don't think we've even seen the tip of this guy's talent.

'He's really gifted. Robert was very focused and attentive during the production of this movie. He is at his best when a lot is demanded of him. I think he is at his weakest when he gets bored. There is a part of him that is very restless, which is easily turned into discontent. The more that is asked of him, the better he performs and this role really did demand a lot. The rehearsal was very fraught, because he was running between the dialogue coach, the writing coach, the oboe coach – he had five or six different coaches. But he is able to absorb a tremendous amount of tasks of pretty high difficulty rating and really nail them. He works very hard to do it – I don't mean it comes easily. To learn to fake playing the baroque oboe is not an easy thing to do. But he pulled it off, better than anyone.'

Of Robert's off-set struggles, Hoffman added,

'Robert is a victim of his own struggles. I'm sure he knows a lot more about debauchery than I ever will, but he wants to better himself. As an actor, he's right on the edge of greatness.'

Sam Neill, who played the King, added, 'Robert and I were kindred souls on the set. We both had the wrong accents. Australians get kidded even more than Americans about our speech. But Robert is the best and bravest of his generation. It takes tremendous courage for a young American actor to take a part like this.'

But the film would be delayed for over a year because of reshoots and poor test reactions. 'The first time they screened this film, the test results came back very, very, very poor and I think that was largely because it was a period film,' said Robert. 'This is not the kind of film that is going to get your *Toy Story* ratings so don't worry about it. I think the people involved in the film got very scared and we went back and reshot these scenes and we tried to fix it. I think by trying to fix a film that didn't need fixing it turned into a big mess. Now, *Restoration* is restored to pretty much what it was. So I'm really pleased with that.

'You know, I think sometimes it's just what is meant to be on a specific film ... it was meant to be the hardest, most frustrating, endless, rewarding, wonderful, scary, laughs-a-minute [experience]. We've been involved in this project for going on eighteen months, you know? That's just a long time. If anyone had been told how long a process this film would be, I don't think a single person in their right mind would have signed on to do it.'

It was a tough, long shoot on the film and Robert found himself in the headlines for verbally abusing his co-star Hugh Grant. 'I just thought Hugh Grant was a dick, that's all,' Robert said. 'And I still do... That could be something that has to do with me, or it could just be that not everyone in this industry is someone I'd care to hang out with.'

Grant would only respond, 'Consider the source. His words say more about him than they do about me.'

Certainly, it was a dark time for Robert. His behaviour was becoming erratic, he was exhausted and he was still unsatisfied that he had fully capitalised on the success of *Chaplin*. Between the making of *Restoration* and its release, he had also made Shakespeare's *Richard III* with Sir Ian McKellen. The fact that such an illustrious actor would wax lyrical about Robert's talents just made him more depressed. He still thought he had nothing to really show for it.

'After I'd been in London working on *Restoration*, I came back to find that Debbie had gone into every bathroom in our house with little baskets and put little rolled up towels and soaps. She knew I'd like it if our house resembled a hotel.'

Robert next starred in *Danger Zone*, a 1996 action-drama that saw him being paid $500,000 to do two weeks' work in South Africa.

Director Allan Eastman said, 'I've worked with Oscar winners and there's absolutely no doubt Robert's the best I've worked with. I was always fascinated to see what he would do. There are a lot of famous actors who are only the characters they play. That's one of their tragic flaws. They have to become something so they can be something. But Robert isn't like that at all. Robert *is* someone. Robert is all the characters he plays, but he's also Robert. And he's a very impressive individual.'

But with both *Restoration* and *Danger Zone* flopping at the box office, he said ruefully, 'I have to watch this but I'm starting to think I'm box-office poison. If you want your film to have a lousy opening weekend just throw me in it, because I've never been in a film that was a big hit.'

10

BREAKDOWN

'His particular case concerns me a great deal,
because he's somebody I know personally and care a
great deal about. I think he is a poster boy for
the fact that prison doesn't cure it'
SEAN PENN

To his fans, Robert Downey Jr was something of a maverick, a heady breath of fresh air, jolting by-the-numbers films into life. Movie industry insiders, however, knew that he was a disaster waiting to happen.

His late-night partying had turned into something far seedier and dangerous. The substances he was taking were used less to keep the party going longer, but as something that he would take by himself or with other like-minded 'friends'. This included taking punk speedballs (crack and heroin together – a potentially deadly mixture) with Hollywood actor Tom Sizemore.

'We did [punk speedballs] basically by ourselves or with each other,' admitted Sizemore. 'It wasn't glamorous. It wasn't out in the open. It was quiet and kind of desperate.'

Robert would say, 'It's so much easier to spend every night out getting drunk with the boys and making a thousand phone calls in pursuit of drugs than to stop and say, "OK, what am I going to do tomorrow when I wake up late and it all just starts over again?" Substance abuse is just a real easy way to give yourself something to do every day. It's something you know you always get the same result from, not trying something different like changing your life – you don't know what the results are going to be then, success or failure. I've never failed to get high from smoking a joint, I've never failed to get depressed from doing coke. Even though there are usually negative outcomes, at least you know it's going to be that same fucking negative every time and it's so comfortable.'

Then, in April 1996, Deborah walked out on Robert, taking their son with her.

'Our marriage and having a child probably kept me from going off the rails completely, but it wasn't enough to right the ship,' Robert said afterwards. 'We started off in high gear. I couldn't maintain the relationship and then she got pregnant. That helped, but even that couldn't deter me from my primary purpose, until now. I realise now with Deb, you can't just have a home base with someone and expect things to work. You can't keep flying out of the nest and coming back with gifts and insight and humour and expect things to last.'

Deborah said, 'I think the wounds with Robert are growing up and repeating the pattern. I think his specific wounds are yet to be revealed to him. They're yet for him to look at... If I thought there was just too much water under the bridge, we would have split a long time ago. There'll never be too much water under the bridge.'

She would later add, 'You can only know a person for how you know them. I have a sadness that we separated, but the process of evolution is always changing. We separated, but we're still connected. But our greatest accomplishment is Indio – that speaks for itself. There's so much love that has come from that... [Robert is] much more into the games and pretending, and I'm more into the adult role. But Indio is definitely his primary focus. It's taken practice for both of us. Of course, sometimes, you just don't want to get up in the morning, but Robert is always pretty game.'

Robert was living his life as an addict. He would have to break out of his own house on a regular basis after friends locked him in for his own safety. He would also hone his skills of duplicity and cunning and would be able to leave the house, score drugs and get back home within 45 minutes.

It was to become a familiar pattern. Concerned, his friends would attempt an intervention – and it was Sean Penn who took the lead. Initially, Penn had been irked by an *SNL* sketch that Robert had done about him, but the pair had since become firm friends. Penn was no stranger to drug and alcohol addiction, and he was desperate to do his best for his friend – even if it meant some harsh measures, including storming into Robert's house and ordering him to go to rehab.

'There's nothing quite as disconcerting as hearing him yell at you through a door about what his intentions were for you that evening,' Robert recalled. 'I just remember waking up, or coming to and saying, "How the hell did he get in here?" He's not to be taken lightly when he's upset. And he was upset.

'And it's so weird when you're trying to break out of your own house. It's that inertia of an addict. The next minute the door flies off the hinges and there's Sean Penn in that leather jacket like, "It's time to pay the piper." I was not out of it enough to put up a fight and I think there was a bit of a struggle on the stairway, which he probably won.

'Then Stephen Baldwin was there and he told me to sit in the back of the car and put my hands where he could see them. A lot of people went to great lengths.

'Next thing I know I'm on a private jet. Then it's three days later and I'm at this treatment centre I've been at before. Everyone's being really nice. The very next thought I had was to escape, to leave the clothes there, take a water bottle. Soon I was fifty miles into the desert – no ID, no cash.'

Robert actually did escape from the facility, adding to *Playboy*, 'Miraculously, I hitched a ride for twenty-seven miles into town, telling them something like, "I'm a married man. I had a room in town and I had" – I just started bullshitting up a storm – "I had a lady of the evening. I woke up and she'd taken my credit cards. I've got to get back to my son's bar mitzvah." I called my accountant in New York, woke him up. Said, "I got to get on a plane now." Next thing I knew, I had a ticket in coach but, because it was me, they bumped me up to first class. Drank the whole hour-and-a-half flight back.'

Not surprisingly, Robert did his best to avoid Penn following his rehab escape. 'After that, he was like, "Forget it." It sucks, too, because someone as honourable as he is, I really should have responded. Jesus, I grew up idolising this guy. Not only does he consider me a friend, but he's taking time. He's got a family. He's got a career that's going well. He's living his dreams and making time for me and I'm like, "I can't, I just can't – sorry, busy."'

Next Robert would once again star with his dad in *Hugo Pool*. The script had been written by Downey Sr's wife Laura, who had died on 27 January 1994 of amyotrophic lateral sclerosis (ALS), a neuro-degenerative disease. 'You never know with ALS when they're going to go,' said Downey Sr. 'The lungs collapse. She was just a kid, thirty-six. She was so loose. And so funny. One time we had a guy in to fix some shelves. He was Russian, he'd been here [in America] two years and he was in the next room and needed to come in where she was. She said, "Don't let him in, cover my legs." "Why?" I asked, "Because *somebody* hasn't waxed my legs for two months. Plus I don't want to make him homesick."'

Robert was very close to Laura and was devastated when she passed away. Downey Sr added, 'She made a very long cassette for my grandson Indio for his twenty-first birthday. My son has it in a safe somewhere out in California.'

When Robert was asked if he was having drug problems during the filming of *Hugo Pool,* he simply replied, 'Yes.'

'It was one of my dad's films. He was trying to help me out and I was just in a bad place. But it's a cult favourite among some of my peers because I was, like, a hundred and thirty-eight pounds and it was beyond improvisation. It's like, "Wow, he's literally bouncing this performance off some space shuttle far away." Which, to tell you the truth, is just another one of my special skills: fencing, archery and acting in a blackout.'

Robert conceded that it was awkward for his parents to see that he was still having problems with drugs. 'It was really weird because my dad was directing it. My cousin was working on the film. It was ouchy and painful for them to see but, again, my work didn't suffer from it. But that didn't mean it was OK. There was a lot of drive for me to seek help.'

Talking about working with his dad on the film, he said, '[It's] another world unto itself. I play a Dutch film director who gets in trouble for shooting an extra and I actually say in the film, "Dank God eet's Los Angeles. I'll probably get off with a leettle commoonity service." Which Dad loved. When I'm doing films with my dad, he knows all the characters I've been doing throughout the years. There are like twenty of them that will come up at any time.'

Hugo Pool was savaged by the critics, with the *Chicago Sun Times* saying, 'An absolutely ridiculous film called *Hugo Pool* will arrive in theatres shortly – and I'm sure it will no doubt very quickly vanish from those theatres in a puff of indifference, because it is monumentally bad.'

The film's mauling didn't faze Robert. His personal problems were a far bigger worry. 'I wanted to stop. I really wanted to. Stopping isn't hard. Not starting again is,' he said.

On 23 June 1996, his black Ford Explorer was stopped by police after going over 70mph in a 50mph speed zone. On searching the car they found cocaine, black-tar heroin and an unloaded handgun – along with four bullets in the glove department.

Robert pleaded no contest to the felony drug possession and possessing the concealed weapon and driving under the influence. He was sentenced to three years probation with requirements of random drug testing and drug counselling. He would say a year later that he was surprised that 'it didn't happen sooner'.

'I ran into Mel Gibson somewhere and he said that he thought it was funny. Yeah. It wasn't funny for me, but to read about the sequence of events, yeah, that's funny. And it's funny because nobody got hurt.

'But I'd have to say that aside from having had a concealed weapon, which was not loaded and which I had a permit for – and by the way, the bullets were where they were supposed to be, which is in the glove box. The only reason they called it a fucking concealed weapon was that it was under the seat. But what am I supposed to do – put it in a gun rack? What's more, I'm in a truck. What am I supposed to do, put it in the flatbed in back and have it rattling around? That would be subtle. Nothing I did deserved punishment or corrective measures or anything. America is fucking ass-backward with respect to a lot of stuff.

'Punishing people for drug dependency. Drug trafficking, maybe. People are dying around that. People are dying around drug dependency too, but look at Holland. It has one of the darkest histories of mankind. But they're not judgemental. I think they're perfectly aware of man's inherent desire to alter his consciousness.'

A month later, things got much worse for Robert. In what would be dubbed the Goldilocks incident, Robert – very much out of it – wandered into a neighbour's unlocked house and passed out on the empty bed where their 11-year-old son normally slept. He was revived by paramedics and spent the night at the USC Medical Centre Prisoners Ward.

'I don't recall [how I got there],' remembered Robert. 'I was trying to justify what happened up and down, saying, "It looked like my house, right?" Then my partner, Joe [Bilella, his partner in the production company Herd of Turtles] laid it on me pointedly that it looked nothing like my house, that there was an elevator that went down into the house.'

The incident has been repeated and retooled as one of those embarrassing things 'Good ol' Robert' got up too when he was high. But in reality, it was a terrifying experience for Bill and Lisa Curtis and their three young children – Daniel, Jenny and Chelsea. Despite their shock, the family didn't press charges against the actor, but Robert was ordered into a supervised drug rehab programme by judge Lawrence Mira.

However, it wasn't long before he again managed to escape. 'Like a velociraptor,' he explained. 'Remember in *Jurassic Park* when they were systematically checking the fence for weaknesses? There were three or four off-duty police officers there, making sure I didn't go anywhere. The mistake that was made, in my estimation, was that I was woken up and given Valium and coffee, which is a low-grade speedball. Then I was alert and relaxed.

'Again, it's so crazy. The thought that went through my head was, "I have to make this a short run." Somewhere in the back of my head, though, I wasn't consciously aware of it. I knew that I had been told, "If you leave here, you are going to jail. The only place you're going from here is jail," and I said, "I don't think so." There was a sweet, dedicated, kind man who I had taken into my confidence. I asked him to get me more coffee while I took a shower. There was one window that opened, so I opened it up and hurdled.

'I'm wearing my hospital pants, a Hawaiian shirt and a pair of slippers and I went into a yacht store and first asked about some boating equipment. That must have been quite a sight. And then I asked the sales guy if he could kindly call me a taxi ... he asked me if I wanted the taxi at the back door. And off I went.'

However, it wasn't long before he was recaptured and held at an LA County jail for nine days. 'I wasn't quite myself yet. So I was talking shit to the people in the jail and saying things like, "Heads will roll." Real pathetic stuff. It was just horrible, being in jail. I wouldn't wish it on anyone.'

He added, 'My mom was pretty much there for the whole thing and I just remember her saying, "Kid, the truth is the truth." I think everybody was fairly relieved that I was in jail for a while, because it's difficult not to sober up in jail.'

On his release Robert was ordered into another supervised rehab program.

He also made a return to *Saturday Night Live*, with one sketch seeing him play a cop who finds a stash of heroin, saying, "In my book if you do drugs, you go to jail and you stay there. You don't go to some cushy rehab centre and take a week off to host some comedy show."

It was getting to the point where Robert was having second thoughts about his career, telling *Playboy* in a 1997 interview, 'I don't give a shit. I love change. I write music. I can paint. I could, by virtue of my semi-celebrity, go out and fucking do a million things, some of which might be a lot more gratifying than acting. I have a love–hate relationship with it because it's so fucking time consuming and usually disappointing. I don't fucking care what happens. I just care how I feel while it's happening.'

Robert was also having money problems. 'Believe me, if ever someone found the transition to boy king an easy one, it was me,' he said in 1997. 'No one ever sat me down and said, "Here's how you build your own little empire." I was very much left to my own devices and, as James Woods said when we were doing *True Believer*, 'This kid has more silk than it took to land the troops in Normandy.' I was way into clothes, way into toys. It was a fad that lasted ten years.

'It was extravagant purchases and no moderation. When we had Indio, we bought a house. I didn't want to be driving around in a Porsche with a baby seat, so we got a Mercedes. Then we wanted a Defender. The Defender had too short a wheelbase – I'd never bothered to test-drive it – so I traded that for a Discovery. Impulsive stuff. But it's just so bothersome to penny-pinch and sit down and go over it all. Now I am more apt to do that because, given my druthers, I wouldn't have done any films this year.'

Still Robert attempted to insist publicly that his problems were behind him and that he was beginning afresh. Tellingly, however, when he appeared on *Prime Time Live*, Diane Sawyer asked him if he was a good liar – to which he replied, 'Yeah, you have to be,' – adding that he was a great liar.

Robert's next movie, 1997's *One Night Stand*, directed by Mike Figgis, would see him give an extremely moving performance as a man dying of AIDS. But there were many incidents around that period which showed Robert was becoming increasingly unstable – including how he got the part for the film.

'Mike was so loving to me, because I was out of my mind when I met him,' he told the media. 'I had a concealed weapon. At the bar. He was looking at me and I'll never forget the look on his face. I was thinking, "What? Is he aware of what's going on?" He asked me, "Why do you have a gun?" It was, like, sticking out of this little purse. I mean, I was completely in a fantasy. I wasn't a badass. I thought I was meeting with Figgis for the handsome-male lead, because I was so debonair. In fact, he was interested in me for the role of the guy dying of AIDS. He gave me the job.'

In a conversation between Robert and Figgis, the director recalled that the actor had been 'barefoot and completely speeding'. 'We had what was, for me, an incomprehensible one-hour meeting and I found myself looking at you and thinking, "You're fascinating, but there are five hundred reasons why you're not going to be in this film." Then, at some point, we started talking about music. I remember driving away and thinking that I'd like you to be in the film, which is what happened. But I could see you were going through a real crisis and it got worse and you were arrested a couple of times while we were making the film. Then you were very well behaved. You never gave me a problem in terms of scheduling, which I thank you for. Then, as we wrapped, you finally got locked up. What was going on?'

Robert replied, 'Well, first up, when I came to meet you at the restaurant, I thought we were going to talk about me playing the lead, which I was perfectly happy with – I was romantic and ready for that assignment. Then, when you said, "No, I think you should play Charlie," I was dying inside. I went in the bathroom to get high and I looked at myself and I said, "You know, I may never look more ready to play someone really sick than I do right now."'

In the event, Robert found the role of a dying man cathartic, saying, 'It was someone whose own proclivities and own sexual promiscuity and own desire to eat life and live fast was the reason that he wasn't going to be there for his friend when he might have enjoyed him most.'

11

ROBERT
BEHIND BARS

*'I chose just to stay out of everyone's
way. It is a scary place'*
ROBERT DOWNEY JR

Insurance – or the inability to find any for Robert –
put paid to him working on *Wild Things*, with the
role going to Matt Dillon instead. It was something
that displeased Kevin Bacon. 'One of the main reasons
I originally wanted to do the picture was that Robert
was involved.' His wife, Kyra Sedgwick, had worked
with Robert on *Heart and Souls*. 'I know Robert and
have a lot of respect for his work,' he said.

Despite missing out on that film, Robert was still
landing roles. 'The first thing I did after was *Two
Girls and a Guy*, with James Toback, who's an old
friend. He gave me my first lead and completely
sympathises with compulsive behaviour.'

Toback said that he got the idea for the movie 'from

watching Downey on TV in an orange smock having been arrested for a second time, looking lonely and isolated and forlorn.'

He added, 'I hope it will not seem too ruthless to confess that my first thought was, "If he can get through this nightmare he will be ready, finally, to become the great actor he has never quite been" – his suffering purging his cuteness, the twisted complexity of his fascinating soul invigorating his dexterous talent. Not too ruthless, because my second thought was, "If Robert finds his way back to physical health, he is going to need a filmmaker to take a risk with him, get him insured, announce to the world ... "He's back!"' And I knew that I wanted to be the one to take that shot.

'So while Robert was in rehab, I was searching for a role, a theme and a story worthy of a reborn entertainer. Duplicity seemed a natural subject. Robert has, after all, been leading at least a double and perhaps a triple life for quite a while. And sexual duplicity seemed an ideally specific form of deception for such a naturally sexual actor.'

The film would tell the story of a guy who is stunned to find the two girls he is dating simultaneously – without each knowing about the other – turning up at his door. The whole aspect of the film would be fast-paced. Toback wrote the script in four days and shot it inside 11. 'I genuinely think that if we'd had a twenty-five-day schedule it would not have worked as well. It forced everyone to get clear and function quickly,' said the director.

In Toback, Robert found a director completely at ease with him, indulging the actor with improvisation and letting him help with the screenplay. When asked to bring something different to the scene, Robert would turn around with an intensely serious face [and say], 'If you really mean that I'll give you some very strange and interesting things.'

Toback added, 'I didn't have long to wait. The next afternoon, the first psychologically crucial scene in the movie was to be shot. Robert, having been caught in "a web of lies and deceit", was to lecture himself in the mirror, to give himself "one more chance" to stop destroying what he cares about. I watched him deliver the lines and was a beat away from calling, "Cut!" when I saw his lips begin to quiver and twitch, his eyes to bulge and his mouth to widen into the limits of its gaping hugeness, at which point he launched into a wild and grotesque send-up of "You Don't Know Me". Voice, eyes and contortions of facial muscles, as well as the cosmic black hole of his mouth, all coalesced into a pure representation of madness. After emitting the final grunts of impacted rage and despair, he collapsed, spent.

'Then he disappeared for a few minutes and returned, ready for the next scene. "Is that what you had in mind?" he asked.'

Heather Graham played one of the two girls in the

movie, and during the short filming schedule it became clear she had an attraction to Robert. 'We're doing this scene and she's basically masturbating me and I'm giving her oral sex for the better part of two or three hours,' Robert recalled. 'Here's what I thought: "I'm really hot and bothered. I hope she's not uncomfortable. Oh well, the day's over." And then I ran into her a year later and she was like, "Why didn't you just call me?"'

Toback added, 'What went on inside the bedroom between Robert and Heather was as close to mutually spontaneous erotic discovery as anything two actors have performed on screen. Only [cinematographer] Barry Markowitz and I were present during the hour, at the end of which both Robert and Heather broke into a joint laughter of relief and release as if to say, "That was fun!"

'You know what Beatty said, when he saw the movie? "This the first time I really felt Downey's sexual power. It's there. I mean, you are a formidable motherfucker here, no question about it."'

Next up was the 1998 thriller *The Gingerbread Man*. While getting the film onto the big screen wouldn't be as eventful as Robert's personal life, it certainly had its dramas. The script, based on John Grisham's story, had been going around the studios without anyone biting. Despite saying that the script was 'generic and had been done before', Kenneth Branagh agreed to make the film if more work was done on the script and if he approved of the director.

In stepped iconic filmmaker Robert Altman, who immediately changed the good-natured protagonist into one who was more cynical and troubled – and added several changes, including a weather storm in place of the original sunny Savannah surroundings. Grisham would leave the project in amicable circumstances – with Altman ruing, 'I never talked to him or met him. I wouldn't know him if he fell in my soup.'

Talking about the script, Robert said, 'When Altman called me about *The Gingerbread Man*, I didn't read it before I said I'd do it. I knew Kenneth Branagh was in it. I loved him. Altman was directing it. There it is. Some say it's haphazard. I think it's haphazard if you're not being intuitive. Still, I am confounded by how you're supposed to do this, build yourself a long-lasting career.'

While Robert was happy to take the part, the studio thought the unquestionably talented but mentally unstable actor was a risky choice to star in the film. A caretaker was therefore enlisted on set to keep Robert out of trouble, something that irked Altman. 'It's obscene and it's barbaric,' he said, 'and it shows that we have no compassion for people with drug problems. He should be in a hospital-care facility ... Robert is a gentle human being, with an illness, an addiction. He has no business being in that place.

'What he did is not a sin, nor is it irregular,' he

added. 'You'd be surprised at the number of people in our industry working every day with a needle in their arm. If I had another role for him right now, I wouldn't give it a second thought to call him on the spot. And I wouldn't ask his people, "So, uh, how's he doing?" How dare we judge him! Everybody should spend more time looking into their own closets.'

Robert loved working with the director. 'It was great, so great. [He] would say things like, "Don't memorise your lines or anything." "Don't look at the script tonight." "That was absolutely adequate, let's move on." Just funny stuff.'

However, after the film failed to satisfy audiences during test screenings, the film was taken out of Altman's hands. Peter Graves, PolyGram's president of marketing, said, 'What happened was nothing out of the ordinary for a commercial film.'

The film's producer Jeremy Tannenbaum said, 'All that really happened was Bob finished a cut and said, "I think I'm through." PolyGram said, "We'd like someone to work with you." Bob said, "No." PolyGram brought in an additional editor and Bob felt betrayed.'

But Polygram's cut fared worse at test screenings – 'I heard there were more close-ups of Branagh and a ridiculous soundtrack,' Altman said – and so they ended up using Altman's cut instead.

Next up for Robert was playing a special agent in *US Marshals*, a follow-up to Harrison Ford's thriller

ROBERT DOWNEY JR

The Fugitive. It's a film that, like *Air America*, Robert is not proud of. 'I don't remember anything about *US Marshals* except that we were running around and pretending like we could ever hold a candle to *The Fugitive*. I just remember like, "Strap on your bulletproof vest, you're in the bayou!" What the fuck? What??

'I did possibly the worst action movie of all time and that's just not good for the maintenance of a good spiritual condition. You've had a traumatic year, you're practically suicidal – what do you think would be really healing for you? How about like twelve weeks of running around as Johnny Handgun? I think that if you talk to a spirit guide, they would say, "That'll kill you."'

Asked why he did the movie, he would add in 1999, 'For the same reason that I did *Air America* ten years before – I thought maybe there was something I was missing and what I really needed to do was to be in one of those films that I love taking my kid to. It would end up being really depressing. I'd rather wake up in jail for a TB test than to have to wake up another morning knowing I'm going to the set of *US Marshals*.'

Robert was aiming to stay clean, however, and his two constant companions in his life were his business partner Joe Bilella and the court-appointed drug counsellor Earl Hightower. Talking about the latter, Robert said, 'Actually, it's been really liberating. We get along and we have a lot of laughs, but we also take care of business. I've never been in this situation, where if something is going on, someone says, "What's up? Let's talk about it." And I actually talk about it.'

His next project was *In Dreams* with director Neil Jordan. 'The role was dark, he was a serial killer, but I just looked at him as someone who had a really bad childhood. He was very childish and I could really relate to that. On that, I probably had six of the best weeks I'd had in a couple of years.'

Robert might have enjoyed working on the movie but when *In Dreams* was eventually released in 1999, it failed to strike a chord with critics. One of the film's co-writers, Bruce Robinson, even said he hated it. In the book *Smoking in Bed: Conversations with Bruce Robinson*, he said, 'What the fuck was Robert Downey Jr, a very fine actor, doing dressed as a nurse cutting people's throats? I didn't know what any of that rushing around was about. Out of the all the things I've been associated with, I hate that the film the most. I think Neil and I should go to the same funeral of this picture and just say goodbye to it gracefully and put a big fucking slab on the top of it.'

But before *In Dreams* could make its brief tour of the cinemas, Robert's life was turned upside down. On 8 December 1997 he was sentenced to 180 days in jail for a parole violation. He would end up spending 118 days in the county jail before he was released for good behaviour.

During that period, he was released temporarily for post-production work on *In Dreams*, something that infuriated Los Angeles County Sheriff Sherman Block. 'Nobody is entitled to special treatment. That is not the way it works in the Los Angeles County jail system.' While allowing that inmates can sometimes attend funerals and for other humanitarian grounds, he argued, 'We do not have releases for people to put finishing touches on films.'

Sheriff Block said, 'I was out at a gathering in South Central Los Angeles and I had at least twenty-five people come up to me and protest that [Downey] was getting special treatment; they know people in jail that don't get that type of treatment.

'Once he comes into our custody, then he's on our playing field and we think people should have to play by our rules,' added Block. 'He's very manipulative, I can tell you that. I hear from people over at the jail [that] he's always trying to con somebody into something.'

However, Robert's lawyer told ABC's *Good Morning America*, 'He was not released from jail for a few hours to do a movie. This was a movie that he had completed before he was sentenced to jail and he was released for a few hours to do some recording of dialogue that had otherwise been destroyed in the course of making the movie. And that was part of an agreement that the judge had entered into with the producers of the movie before Robert Downey was sentenced to jail.

'Understand, while he was on probation – this is a while back, some six or nine months ago – he obviously, during that three-year period, would have to work. But he couldn't work unless the production companies were assured that he would be allowed to finish the job. And the judge did, appropriately, give these companies that assurance.

'He [Robert] was not paid for this and it was not done for his benefit. It was done because of an agreement that the court had with the production company so that, during the period that he was on probation, he would be allowed to work.'

Robert also insists that he was told by a warden, 'If we have any discipline problems with you, we're going to come down on you like a ton of shit.'

Director Curtis Hanson added, 'He told me that when he's in the food line, there's always somebody going, "How come Downey got a bigger portion?" He tries to avoid preferential treatment because there's always somebody trying to stir things up.'

Robert was also attacked by other inmates while in prison. A source told the *Mirror*, 'He is a very frightened man. This was a horrible attack by two men.

'Some sort of row broke out in the kitchen at around eleven am. Within seconds it led to a brutal assault and Robert was punched and kicked. The warders managed to pull the two thugs off him. But he still sustained serious facial injuries. It looks like his nose has been broken and he has two deep cuts to his face.'

His lawyer said, 'It was an attack on Robert Downey. They were shaking him down, some inmates there, as they do. Jail is a hellish place. It's a bad place to be under any circumstances and it's a very bad place to be if you're the focus of other people because you're a celebrity. And so other inmates were taking advantage of that and shaking him down. At one point, another inmate went over and just beat the devil out of him and cut him up pretty bad. He had to be taken from the jail to a plastic surgeon to repair some of the damage.'

After that Robert was taken to solitary confinement, where he had to hang leftover prison luncheon meat high enough so the rats couldn't get to it. 'After I got in the fight I was down in this discipline module, which is like a hole,' he said. 'Three times a day, you see a pair of hands and some food comes in – it's pretty awful.

'One day it opens and there was this lieutenant, with some deputy he's brought by to meet me. I hadn't had a shower in five days, I was sleeping in my clothes [and] my hair was all fucked up. But that Hollywood big-shot entertainer thing came in and I thought, "Well, I'd better come to – I have company." And this guy came in and said, "Listen, I know you don't have a lot to read in here. I hope I wouldn't be crossing the line if I brought a script by for you. It's about unicorns. It's not what you think – there's a very human element to it." And I was just dumbfounded. I said, "Wow, great!"

'There were other times [when] inmates said, "We should do a movie about this." I've heard this from other people too – actors, directors, writers and in some mundane situation like driving school. "Man, we should do a film about this, where we're all in driving school together. It'd be fucking great." Just the last thing you need.

'I chose just to stay out of everyone's way. It is a scary place. The closest I can come to describing the experience is that it must be like active military service. It is very unpredictable and your life is very much at risk. Everybody's life is at risk there, because everybody in there is dangerous. I became as dangerous as I could, considering the environment.

'You're allowed to listen to music in jail, as long as you use headphones. I had some CDs sent to me when I was inside, but the one that was released when I was doing time was Sting's album *Brand New Day*. I derived a lot of comfort from that. It was kinda ironic, though, to be singing along to *Brand New Day* when every brand new day you were still in the pen.'

In March 1998, after serving almost four months of his sentence, Robert was released. Clearly delighted to be out, he vowed that his time behind bars had changed him.

12

BEHIND BARS
ONCE MORE

*'He's a great artist and a great friend and when
he beats this, he's going to be a great man'*
ROBERT DOWNEY SR

Robert was broke. According to *Newsweek*, the IRS had lodged tax liens totalling over $1million against his income throughout the 1990s. His countless designer suits had been given away – or in some cases buried in his garden from his headier partying in the 1980s – and he was now sleeping on the couch of friends.

He would spend from 11.30am to 2.30pm every day working on his first script, and he would make appearances in other films, such as the relationships drama *Friends & Lovers* and the Steve Martin comedy *Bowfinger*. But despite being one of the best technical actors around, he wasn't happy with his work. 'If you woke me up in the middle of the night and said, "Do you want to do this any more?" I'd say, "No."

'It's just enough to keep all the plates spinning. And that's fucking miserable. Right now I have this idea of doing some paintings and putting a little piece of music to each painting for an exhibit. But how can I survive, following that dream?'

One answer was to team up with director James Toback again for 1999's *Black and White* – a film that famously saw him put himself in harm's way. The movie consists of a number of loosely interwoven stories; the link is a married pair of film-makers who are making a documentary about white teenagers attracted to Harlem's hip-hop scene.

Toback explained, 'When Mike [Tyson] got out of prison, I told him I was starting this movie called *Black and White*, which I was going to collaborate on with the Wu-Tang Clan. He got all excited and wanted to do it. Downey had also just gotten out of rehab or jail. My intuition is that interesting people are more interesting right after they have suffered. It opens them up even further. I felt that both of them would be very good in the movie and good together.

'I asked Downey what he wanted to play and he said, "Why don't I play the gay husband of Brooke Shields?" I said, "Good. Why don't you play the gay husband of Brooke Shields who hits on Mike Tyson?" It only occurred to Downey at the last minute to ask whether I had told Mike that he was going to hit on him. I said, "No." Downey said, "What if he gets angry?" I said, "I would assume he would." He said, "How far do you want me to take it?" I said, "Take it until he responds in the extreme." Downey responded, "What if he kills me?" I said, "Well, I haven't thought about that. I think it's unlikely – no better than a five per cent chance. But, at the rate you're going, you're going to end up dying in the parking lot of a motel in Culver City. So what would be better ... that or dying like this?" Downey cracked up and proceeded to provoke Mike at great lengths.'

Shaking with rage, Tyson smacked the actor in the face – Robert said that a slap from the boxer was like being hit with a shovel. He then grabbed Robert round the throat, slammed him on the ground and called him a 'cum drinker'.

Next up and in much safer surroundings, would be the college drama *Wonder Boys* – a film that would see something of a return to form for Robert, playing a has-been book editor alongside Michael Douglas's English professor whose life is falling apart. Director Curtis Hanson had warmed to Robert during a long meeting with the actor before giving him the part.

Although he wasn't playing the main character, Robert noted the similarities to his own situation: 'For three days [Michael Douglas' character] can pretty much drink and take pills and smoke pot and make huge mistakes and in the midst of all that he still has this genuine talent.

'The film has a real poignancy. You can experience that *Wonder Boys* phenomenon regardless of what generation you're in. It reminds me of people in the 1980s who were living high off the hog in New York and LA. They were at all the clubs and had all the new clothes and so on. Now, ten years later, they're still wearing the same stuff and still trying to ride on the same coat tails, except that it's just not working any more. They really haven't done anything for ten years.'

But after the film was made, Robert violated his parole again. 'It breaks my heart,' said Douglas. 'Robert is fantastic. He was great in the movie and is, without doubt, the best and most extraordinary actor in my country. Near the end, I was really worried. He was in the middle of marital difficulties – he had no home back in Los Angeles.

'All the signs were there for possible problems. There were all the signals that he was going to be at loose ends again after the filming of *Wonder Boys*.'

Because of the parole violations, Robert was ordered to court. It seemed another jail sentence was very likely, but Robert wasn't going to go down easy. He had another performance still in him. Before sentencing, he famously told the court, 'It's like I've got a shotgun in my mouth and I've got a finger on the trigger and I like the taste of the gun metal.'

Robert Shapiro, who had been OJ Simpson's defence attorney, stated, 'This is a person suffering from a disease he can't control. Even the dire threat of jail or prison is not enough of a deterrent.'

However, Judge Mira was not moved, saying, 'I don't think we have any alternative. We have used them all.' He then shook Robert to his core by sentencing him to three years in jail.

'It felt like a death sentence, like he might as well have uttered some Latin spell over me and cast me into Hell,' said Robert.

Stunned and visibly shaken, Robert was taken to prison. 'I was like, "What the Dickens am I doing here?" I wasn't so much scared as in shock. A symptom that characterises the first phase is shock. Under certain conditions, shock may even precede the prisoner's formal admission into the camp. The main symptom of the second phase is apathy, a necessary mechanism of self-defence.

'I thought it would be a lot smaller and tame. I was like, "Oh my God – what the fuck?" I thought it was going to be, like, the Corcoran State Prison and Theme Park and I was fucking speechless.'

In fact, the prison was in the middle of nowhere, stuck in the middle of the vast Californian wasteland. 'In the winter it feels like you've landed on the surface of the moon. It's so desolate and sterile and depressing,' said *Wonder Boys* director Hanson.

Douglas said he and Hanson were 'heartbroken' when they heard that Robert was going to prison. 'Initially, I was so mad at him – it's such a terrible disease. I think he was sober on the set – he was so great to work with. I'm deeply fond of him. In his sobriety, you can sense how painful simple alertness is for him. He feels it all – watching him, you can understand the notion of self-medication. There's a vulnerability about him that makes you want to protect him. I sure hope he gets himself squared away. I guess we'll have to wait for the next chapter.'

Hanson said, 'I found his mental state to be surprisingly good, given the circumstances. There seemed to be an attitude of acceptance, if you will – an acceptance of responsibility, which made me think that he will get through the situation.'

One inmate would remember, 'Robert kept to himself at first. He tried dealing with it like a monk, which is one way of doing it.'

But visits from his son would break his heart. 'I feel so guilty that Debbie is now additionally accountable to Indio. I just feel so awful about that,' he commented.

Debbie said, 'Indio doesn't care if Robert is a hero. He just wants to love and be loved back. Robert wanted to tell him how he was going off to Yugoslavia to learn how to be a spy. And I said, "No, that's not right – tell him the truth." So he did. It's thrown Indio for a loop – he gets quiet and doesn't like talking about it. But Robert's been gone many times before – working on a film, in rehab, so he's used to that. Jail, for Indio, is what he sees in the movies.

'I'm angry at Robert. But I'd never use Indio as a weapon. Robert and I will always be connected through him.'

Robert's dad said, 'Hollywood is a horrible place. Life is too easy when you're a movie star. People will do anything you want and get you anything you want. The truth is, if he hadn't been sent to prison, he'd probably be dead by now.'

Sean Penn said, after he visited his friend in prison, 'His humour was well intact. He seemed like a guy doing time, one day at a time. Robert's always been a hard read, though, because of his sense of humour. It's difficult for someone to say something as silly as, "Boy, he's doing great!" But given that, he looked great and he made me laugh a lot.

'I felt that a sentence was needed – something had to happen – but now it's entering what you'd call cruel and unusual punishment. We need Robert Downey Jr free! We need him, just selfishly speaking, as an actor. His talent raises that bar. And the bar has dropped so low ever since they put him behind bars.'

Robert worked on kitchen duty, working five days a week from 4.30 to 8pm, making eight cents an hour. His duties would include handing out the food to his fellow inmates and washing dishes.

'I was pots-and-pans man in the kitchen tonight,' he said. 'That's the fucking real deal. There was pizza, pasta and spinach. And so we had about seventy-five very large, impossible fucking pizza pans to deal with.

It was fucking genius! I'm, like, in a fucking disposal. There's three sinks that are the size of a truck, all filled with piping-hot water and stuff called Dish-All.'

He remembered one time where bags full of gravy burst everywhere and another when he was floating in gallons of garbage water. 'Like five hundred pounds of slop. It is at these moments – these points of acceptance – that you realise that human beings can do fucking anything.'

Dubbed 'Mo Downey' by his cellmates, Robert again found himself getting into physical scrapes with other inmates, who were desperate to make a name for themselves. 'They were trying to muscle me into giving some sort of pay-off for protection and I said, "When I'm done reading the Stephen King novel, I'll come over and we'll talk shop." But you don't come out with that in jail, because the next thing I knew, it was on. And, well, it was cool after that – they didn't fuck with me.'

An inmate named Mike, who befriended Robert, remembered one potentially nasty incident concerning a racquetball game and a 'guy with a chip on his shoulder, who's at least two people wider than Downey.

'He started coming at Downey, banging into him, calling him stuff and Downey's like, "Hey, you don't have to talk like that," and I'm whispering to Downey, "Don't say another word to him, man!" Next thing I know they're, like, walking toward each other. Downey just doesn't take any shit. And

162

Downey will start to walk away and the guy keeps saying things to piss Downey off. Finally, I convinced the guy that he didn't want to get more months added to his time and he backed off.

'They can say Downey is protected, but like with everyone else, it's a false sense of security because you never know if the guy next to you is going to break your neck in the middle of the night when you're sleeping. That's something they can't prevent. There's always the danger element. What's the probability factor? That nothing's going to happen to him. However, fate is fate. So they're saying he's in prison for his own good, but any day could be his last. That's the way it is.'

According to Robert, he was threatened again when Mike left. 'He goes, "So what are you gonna do now that Mike is gone?" And I said, "Your head games never had any effect on me when Mike was here. What makes you think that they're going to now?"' That ended that incident.

Robert's cellmate Figueroa Slim added, 'You know, some of the guys in here think he's the Bank of America. They try, you know, to, like, take advantage.'

After *Vanity Fair* pressed questions about possible sexual assault, Downey said, 'What I hear is that, if you're on a lifer yard, it's perfectly respectable, to some, to partner up with another inmate. I can neither confirm it nor deny it.'

Later in the interview he added that he 'would

never tell you the worst things that have happened to me'.

Robert spent large parts of his day in isolation, on the top bunk of cell number 17. The prison yard was his backdrop. But he would look at the shrine he had made and taped to his wall, full of letters and photographs and newspaper and magazine clippings. About a hundred letters would be sent to him every week – most from admiring females he had never met. He would attempt to respond to as many of them as he could and would send friends his artwork, which were drawn with crayons and markers on anything that he could find – papers bags or envelopes. He would attempt to sell the artwork to his celebrity friends.

His mother mentioned the irony that it took her adult son to go into prison before he really got close to her. 'Whatever it takes, I guess. [He wrote me] the most beautiful poem. I'm just so pleased to hear from him so often now – however I can get it. I hang on to every word he writes me, like it was, you know, the law. I pay close attention to what he's saying. The love is there, for sure.'

Allyson added, 'It's the first time ever, I think, that he's remembered my birthday. He made me a card. It was November 29. He's writing to me all the time.'

His wife would say, 'It's good if he's not feeling as if he's got to be "on" all the time. That's what is going to save his life – to be truthful, to not always be covering something up. What I most wish for him is that he finds a simple way of living.'

Robert found simplicity of a kind, though not that imagined by Debbie. He would regularly get sent care packages – filled with turkey, rice, pasta and Irish Cream coffee. Every week he and his cellmates – Slim (Charles Bell), Timmons, Sugar Bear and Big Al – would take all the leftovers from packages sent to them and they'd share them in a picnic.

Looking back later, Robert would say, '[Jail is] an unimaginably awful situation. What you have to do is protect yourself and amuse yourself in that order. In a way, I think I felt like I was in this dangerous, monastic boot camp. I don't complain on film sets so much now.'

But outside the prison, Robert's close friends hadn't quite given up on him. A huge support campaign was growing for Robert, calling for his release. Their wishes were finally granted and in August 2000 he was released, three months earlier than expected. This came about after his lawyers had successfully argued that his three-year sentence had been wrongly handled by Judge Mira, who had said, 'I'm going to incarcerate you in a way that's very unpleasant for you.'

In his attempt to duck the press upon his release from his jail, Robert was led out of the back and sped away to LA, where he changed cars after pulling into a car wash. He then headed to a 12-step meeting.

'I'm proud of the way I've conducted myself since the incarceration and proud of the choices I've made since I've been released,' he told *Details*. 'The threat of prison has been eliminated for me. I know I can do time now. I can even go out and do stuff that makes what I did before seem tame and then go handle my business wherever they would put me. Practically all the fear about that has been eliminated.

'I'm coming from a place of total strength and humility now. A couple of days after I got out, I called the guy who would be my parole officer, told him I felt a little weird in that I was out on bail. I told him if there's anything you want me to do, even before we start, tell me and I'll do it.'

He added, 'I can't tell you what a pleasure it is just to take a nice shower. It's so cool – using a hair dryer again, good towels – and I can lock the door if I want.

'It's real simple. I'm a lot more ready to listen to folks who have been through this as opposed to thinking, "I'm more complex, I'm an artist."'

His addiction counsellor, Warren Boyd, told *Details*, 'I don't like to make predictions, but I can tell you that the recovery that Robert demonstrates – the way he walks and talks – I've seen few people fail when they're like that. When he was released, he could have gone anywhere. The first thing he wanted to do was go to a meeting.'

Again Robert came out of jail broke, and now Debbie, the woman in his life, was legally separated from him and living with another man. 'I was an asshole, a total asshole,' Robert told *Details*. 'And basically, this is all my fault.

'I so appreciate the simple things now. When I got out, I stayed in this middle-class house with a boat and a muscle car. I had a little room. It was the kind of place where I used to say, "OK, I can rough it here for two days." Now it was like, "Wow, I've got my own bathroom! The toilet has a lid and it isn't made of metal!"

'Chemicals were the last addition to an entirely bloated dysfunction. For me, it was about women and spending. The drugs were the icing, part of the deal. They all worked together. I was clearly thinking I needed this stuff. What I'd worked out was a way to imagine I could do the wrong things the right way. That I could manage abusing drugs. I knew it wasn't really going to pan out, but I wasn't allowing myself the chance to realise the joy of living to prevent it.'

Robert's celebrity friends were overjoyed at his release. 'I think he's going to make it. I pray for that,' said Tom Sizemore.

Sean Penn: 'He said that he hasn't used in prison. I choose to believe him, although I'll admit I've been fooled before.'

James Toback: 'He's a sweet guy who never did harm to anyone except himself. He's been doing drugs for twenty years and functioning for twenty years and in those twenty years there've been hundreds of people who've been getting high constantly and behaved very destructively and have not been arrested. Robert's real problem is he gets caught.'

Michael Douglas added, 'He got a bad judge. Robert had had some incidents before. There's a certain philosophy in our penal system – after you've tried to solve the problem three times through rehabilitation, then you try to punish them.

'Some statistics have proved that "hard" prison rehabilitates faster than any other kind, but nobody anticipated anywhere the amount of time Robert was given. He turned himself in for rehab and the judge pulled him out. But he didn't hurt anybody. He didn't do anything at all.'

Robert, however, saw things somewhat differently. 'I just loved it when people said, "Well, he's not hurting anyone but himself." I liked that so much that I ran with it for a while. But it's so not true. Drug abuse is wrong. It's not OK. I let down everyone who ever cared about me.'

Once again he was saying all the right things. But Robert is one of the greatest actors of his generation. Was this just another of his best performances?

13

ROBERT ON THE
SMALL SCREEN

*'I never expect to have an impact on anything, except
perhaps a brick wall at a hundred miles an hour'*
ROBERT DOWNEY JR

After Robert was released, he found that
Hollywood hadn't forgotten him. His publicist
Alan Nierob said, 'I think he'll resume working as he
was before he was incarcerated. His talents have
always been in demand and I see no reason for that
to change.'

People may have been more wary of hiring him, but
he still found work – even if it was work he might
have turned down in the past. This was particularly
true of his role in the long-running TV show *Ally
McBeal*. 'I always thought it was inventive and cool,'
he said. 'But to tell you the truth, I would have been
happy upon getting to do an In-n-Out [fast-food

chain] commercial. I'd been a bit of a snob about TV and it was just another thing I was wrong about.'

The show – about quirky lawyer Ally McBeal, played by Calista Flockhart – had been an instant success, but in its third year ratings began to drop. So when fate played its hand by securing a hugely talented actor looking for any kind of break, the programme's makers almost bit it off. 'We're thrilled,' the show's creator, David Kelly, announced. 'We've admired his work for years and know he'll make an enormous contribution to the show.

'It just smelled like a really good match,' he continued. 'Robert has this comedic tone that I thought was really organic to our show. We've had a very hard time finding love interest for Ally and one of the reasons is that when you see Ally with a guy you just sort of [go], "Uh-oh, he's not going to make it." I think our audience is extremely protective of Ally – as we are – so whoever she's dating, he'd better be good enough.'

'I think he's inspired people to go the extra mile,' said Flockhart of Robert's arrival. 'It's hard doing a show for four years. You get into patterns, you get into ways of doing things and everybody just kind of… I don't want to imply that things weren't good before, but the energy of somebody new coming in sends in a little *zwuushhh*… sweet inspiration. Maybe he raised the bar a little bit.'

Robert would say of his co-star, '[She] is the crème

de la crème of actresses. There's an ever-unfolding – I don't want to say repartee – but kind of subliminal commentary going on. She's so fast and she's so freakin' smart that I can go somewhere with her and then she'll read that and take it down some Stuttgart side alley, somewhere weird, you know what I mean?'

Robert added, 'David's a genius and Calista's awesome.' He even found time to poke fun at the time he spent in prison by adding, 'Once again I have a choice of shirt colours.'

After his release Robert had checked into an outpatient treatment centre in Huntington Beach, but after two months he moved into a two-bedroom apartment in Hollywood that is best described as modest. He would turn up at 6am to work on *Ally McBeal*, attending 12-step meetings held on the studio lot, organised by the show's bosses.

Flockhart raved, 'Whenever he comes into the room and we begin the scene, you just know that something is going to happen. He's not an actor that's going to be bullied into conformity. There's just something so uninhibited and so free and so uncensored about him. And he's unequivocally bright and smart, so that combination is deadly.'

Director Bill D'Elia said, 'I was fortunate enough to direct the first scenes with those two and it felt like I was back in the 1940s, making an old romantic comedy.'

In fact, Robert was romantically linked to

MARTIN HOWDEN

Flockhart, but she would later end up with Harrison Ford. 'Once Harrison came on the scene that was it, but I tell myself not many guys can compete with Harrison Ford,' quipped Robert.

His appearance saw ratings of the show in the US go up by 11 per cent. Fox Entertainment president Gail Berman raved, '[*Ally McBeal*] is back to its glory. If it was ever off, it's certainly back now.'

Even Robert's son was impressed, seeing his dad play a good guy. The show's costume designer, Kathleen Detoro, said, 'I often saw them playing together in the hallways. Robert was very affectionate to his son.'

Ally McBeal producer Pam Wisne told *Details*, 'We knew he would have good chemistry with Calista Flockhart. He agreed and it worked out well. The cast loves him, the crew loves him. We would love for him to stay beyond the eight episodes, for as long as he wants.'

But, despite all the mutual admiration, Robert would later tell the *New York Times*, 'I was also very, very unhappy – unhappy at that point in my life, but also with the whole TV thing. There is no way out of a series until your contract is up. It was like *Groundhog Day* being on that.'

He would add, 'Do you know what it's like to come straight out of jail and onto *Ally McBeal*? I was still wondering if we were playing handball in the prison yard at lunchtime. They asked me if I was going to be

172

OK while offering $115,000 a week. I just nodded. There were others on the show in recovery and they knew I wasn't going to be OK. It just got out of hand. But I gave them a good run, seven or eight episodes before I got high again. Then all that goodwill went out the window and they asked me to take urine tests while someone watched. But who did they think they were messing with? They couldn't threaten me with a urine test after all I'd been through. I found some fake piss. I'm the green beret of liars! It doesn't matter what you say to me, I'm going to nod, smile and then get loaded.

'It was a brilliant mistake. I never expect to have an impact on anything, except perhaps a brick wall at a hundred miles an hour. So it was cool again. I mean, where had I been? I'd just gotten out of the pen. I wasn't thinking about me and Ally McBeal, I was thinking, "Dude, I've got eight pairs of pants. Let's go to the gym. I look good, everyone likes me, where's all this pussy?" And what happened, you know? One more time, damn the torpedoes. It was all set up to be mutually beneficial – it was only my inability to see the truth of what [it was] that sent me down off the wrong track again.'

As before, just when things were going well, Robert found a way to ruin it. It all started when his aspiring screenwriter friend, Mark Miller, agreed to Robert's request to spend Thanksgiving weekend with him at the Merv Griffin Resort – a very expensive hotel in

Palm Springs. Robert had waved the glossy brochure at him, saying, 'Dude, just come.'

Initially dismissing the idea as 'boring', Miller relented after deciding the trip could be one where they could work on their many screenplay ideas. 'We might have been the Matt Damon and Ben Affleck of our time – if we'd done it ten years ago when we were in London,' Miller told *Rolling Stone*. (Miller had stayed with Robert while they were working on *Chaplin*.)

Certainly, Robert had screenwriting aspirations. 'My dad used to say, "Why don't you go change the world? Go out and make a movie,"' Robert said.

In fact, he got as far as writing a script with Anthony Hall called *Seth and McGuigan* – 'It's about two guys in a rehab centre. Something happens so they can't get out and it's about what they do looking for happiness in every area of life.'

Robert also had ideas about a high-school-reunion drama, a thriller set in Las Vegas in the 1960s, and *Dan's Best Friend*, a drama about a narcoleptic dog walker. 'It's a big ensemble. It's kind of dark,' he would say.

Things began well. The $600-a-night hotel room offered luxurious surroundings and work began promisingly on their screenplay, but the next afternoon Robert began to get restless. Knowing the dangers that could follow when that happened, Miller decided to take him to a nearby strip club. 'Sex would be the best alternative to drugs,' he reasoned. 'I don't mean that we were going to find sex, but to be in the environment of sex might take his mind off drugs.'

The night started with Robert Downey Jr heading to the strip club Show Girls wearing a Nike baseball cap, rumpled jacket, baggy black trousers and white trainers, blending in with the working class clientele, while Miller stood out with bright green leather pants and a green turtle-neck.

One of the dancers, Laura Burnett, said, 'Mark was the stuck-up one. Robert was down to earth. He asked us how we liked our work and what we did for the holiday. He told me that he missed his son.'

Within minutes he was mobbed by fans and dancers – including a 21-year-old woman called Kiley Ridge, who had turned up at the venue to pick up her final pay cheque as a cocktail waitress. Spotting Robert, she plucked up the courage to ask him for an autograph for her brother Mike, who had turned up with her. After he gave her his signature, she whipped off his hat and placed it on her hair – an almost ironed-out hairstyle that resembled the TV character Dharma, after whom Kiley had been nicknamed. It wasn't long, she said to *Rolling Stone*, before she was told by Robert, 'I want to leave with you right now.' 'I was like, "Oh my God! Robert Downey Jr wants to leave with me and I forgot to shave my legs."'

Miller, who was not a drug user, claimed that, while he lectured Robert about his addiction, 'Robert will excommunicate you if you are just ragging on him like people in the AA programme do.'

Despite accusations that he did more harm than good – 'A friend like Mark is a blessing to the disease and a curse to the person who has it,' said Tom Sizemore – Miller said, 'There may be some truth I was an enabler. [But] I love Robert with all my heart. Why weren't Robert's other friends with him at a time when he was alone, going through a divorce? Why were they ignoring him and letting him fall apart?' Fearing an 'imminent danger' Miller phoned a friend, saying that he was having trouble keeping him in check. 'We thought it was best for him to settle down and think about what he wants to achieve, to think about staying sober, to think about being productive. We told him we would fight this together.'

However, their intervention was caught out when Laura Burnett turned up with another stripper and they went to a Mexican restaurant, where the stripper who had the Dharma-style hair also turned up. At the restaurant, Robert was once again besieged by autograph hunters desperate to be seen with the actor, and there were unsavoury well-wishers offering to do drugs with him in the toilet.

Back at the hotel, Miller and his friend persuaded the dancers to leave and told the hotel not to send any more alcohol to Robert's room or permit cash advances on his credit card. Confident that they had averted any more trouble for Robert, Miller headed back to LA on the Saturday afternoon.

But across town, trouble was brewing. An anonymous caller to police from a pay phone not far from the Show Girls strip club said, 'In Room 311 of the Merv Griffin Resort there is a man that is with an ounce of cocaine and a couple of guns and is pretty upset.'

When officers turned up to Robert's room they found more than five grams of cocaine and methamphetamine. A police spokesman said, 'He was cooperative and, in our opinion, under the influence of a controlled substance. He was charged with that. He invited the officers into the suite and we continued the search. Throughout the entire incident he was compliant.'

Robert is said to have pleaded with the cops, saying, 'Don't do this to me. You're going to ruin my life.'

'He seemed very sad, very, very subdued,' said the hotel manager. 'I heard him say that he needed to get to work on Monday.'

The manager also stressed that Robert had been no trouble. 'I greeted him when he arrived. He was friendly, very nice. He kept very private. He behaved normally – no ruckus, no parties, no noise.'

Robert couldn't believe his bad luck. Nor could the makers of *Ally McBeal* – it's said that the show's creator was furious with Robert because the season was developing the couple's slow-burn romance. After

Robert's exit from the show, the producers turned to Dame Edna Everage in a bid to save falling ratings.

Meanwhile, Robert's publicist, Alan Nierob, said, 'He is working very hard and is extremely dedicated to his rehabilitation and his sobriety. 'He is doing very well, taking this upon himself to do this. That's always a good sign.'

In the end Robert was sentenced to 12 months in a live-in rehabilitation centre and 3 years' probation. It meant that his roles would soon dry up. Before the drug incident, he was offered a role in *America's Sweethearts*, but director Joe Roth said, 'I don't know what's going to happen. It's heartbreaking that this happened. We're trying to sort it out now. We don't want to hurt him in any way, but we have to figure out what we'll do for our movie.' Needless to say, it didn't happen.

Downey added, '*Ally McBeal* was my bottom, those last couple of rungs. The impulse at that point was not even acting out any more. It was not like, "I'm thinking about tying one on and pretending that it will still be fun." It was more like the arm's been cut off, but the phantom limb is twitching.'

He would go on to say, 'Here is something people who don't take drugs often forget: No one takes drugs because he wants to break the law, or end his marriage, or wind up crusty and homeless. People take drugs because drugs make them feel better. And some people have a deeper need to feel better than others.'

14

GIBSON LENDS A HELPING HAND

'The movie saved my ass in so many ways'
ROBERT DOWNEY JR

Robert was allowed out of rehab to appear in a music video for Elton John's moving ballad 'I Want Love', which would see Robert lip synch to the song.

Elton said, 'I wanted to do a video that was mature. And [director] Sam Taylor-Wood said, "I've got an idea of just doing it very simply: one person – not you – lip-syncing to the song. An actor, maybe." I came up with the idea of Robert. I thought, "God, the lyrics are very close to home. I wonder if he'll do it?" He was very interested. We sent him the album and he said, "Yes."

'It all came together in five or six days. I'm thrilled with it. I don't necessarily think an artist has to be in a video. On the other singles that we do videos for, I'm going to ask people that don't normally make videos to interpret the songs, whether they use me or not. This one worked perfectly, because I was able to stay in France on holiday while Robert was doing it! I love the fact that it is a one-shot video. He did sixteen takes. They used the very last take because he was completely relaxed by then. It's so pertinent to what he's going through and the way he underplays it is fantastic.'

Following the video's success, an old friend came calling. As Robert recalled, '[Mel Gibson] leaves me this message: "I know you don't like hearing this, but I've got this role for you. It's about you. And you're playing it. Can't pay you much. Gimme a call to find out when we start."

'Mel came over to the pad and, in addition to making me whatever – I don't know, a green avocado bioflavonoid soup shake – he said, "You might want to check this out; I just bought the rights to it." I thought, "Does he think I need something to do this weekend?" I said, "OK. What for?" He said, "For us to do, whatever. I gotta split." You turn around and he's taking off on a chopper somewhere.

'I'd hate it if he turned on me,' he added. 'I'd lose it.'

The script was for *The Singing Detective* – a remake based on the acclaimed BBC mini-series written by Dennis Potter. The film's director, Keith Gordon, who had acted with Robert on *Back To School*, described it as 'your basic comedy-drama surrealist 1950s lip-synching rock 'n' roll musical absurdist expressionist film-noir pastiche naturalist character study'. Robert was to play the disfigured central character, writer Dan Dark, memorably played in the original by Michael Gambon.

Or, as Robert put it, 'Well, after everyone else turned it down and it fell into my lap and after they had been through all the other directors who were inappropriate for it and Keith [Gordon] had been chasing it and after Katie [Holmes] said, "Well, actually, I'm busy and have a real career, but I'm always happy to do community service with the riff raff."'

Gibson said, 'I knew he could do it. Especially the suave part. No doubts about it, Gambon was tremendous. He made himself handsome just through attitude – that's a great actor but so is Robert... I just want to work with people I like and he's one of them. Also, every two weeks I send him a Polaroid of my cock laying across a chopping block.'

Downey would call Gibson 'like a big brother who plays tricks on you.

'However, what made me want to do it after a while was Keith telling me that that this was going to be something that I could enjoy. This would be something that didn't have to drain me and be one more time of, "Here we are." And it seemed like it's gonna be a small film that had artistic value and you go, "Oh my God, please just let me do fifteen action movies – these little art films kill you!" But it's neither. It turned out to be something that I think is good to watch regardless of what your opinions – and we know everyone's got one – are. Not only did we have a good time, we are all better soldiers having involved ourselves in this.'

Tackling a topic that would become a recurring theme in Robert's latest comeback, Gordon said, 'Basically, Mel was the insurance. Robert was uninsurable at the time, although I think he is now since he's proven he's back, he's clean and he's doing good. This whole thing is really Mel giving a gift to someone he loved as a person and believed in as an artist.'

Katie Holmes, who played Nurse Mills, said, 'Everyone who meets him just cares about him. We're all rooting for him.

'I felt a lot of freedom on the set. I was very intimidated to work with Mr Downey. I don't know why! It was so exciting and it's just so fun to work with people who change so much in every take but it's so real. It was very inspiring as a young person, as a new actor, and Keith did let us try many different things. I had a wonderful, wonderful time.'

When pressed on why she found Robert intimidating, Holmes admitted, 'He would just embarrass me to death. So quick-witted that most of what he said went right over my head.'

During filming Robert had to be covered in make-up to represent the skin condition. He said, 'If we had a twenty-minute break, I would go get my [tennis] racquet and go out in the make-up, and I'd go play up against the side of the stage. You know, just to get my cardio. I didn't care if I'm in the make-up, or whatever I'm doing. I have to maintain my sanity. So I would go. And it would help the make-up come off too, because you'd start sweating underneath.

'But we weren't shooting really privately – we were trying to get something that was affordable. But in effect, there were the food-service people milling around and I'd be just like... getting my sweat on! I freaked some people out.'

Talking about the various demands made on him by the role, he added, 'In order of comfort, I was most comfortable being tarred and feathered! I was less comfortable with the song and dance. And I was wildly uncomfortable with the cool detective guy stuff.

'All I had to do was not blow it. And stay sane. Which isn't that difficult! Lately. But the song-and-dance stuff was about physicality. And it's been a long time since I'd been called to the hierarchy of physicality. Since *Chaplin*, really.'

Gordon compared the Robert he had worked with on *Back to School* to the current version. 'He was all manic energy then, not that he doesn't have a lot now. But now there's this deep intelligence from someone who is very deep, both emotionally and intellectually. It's actually a wonderful marriage, because he still has all the energy of a nineteen-year-old.'

No stranger to comebacks, Robert was nonetheless confident that this time would be different. It helped that Gordon was exactly the type of director that Robert wants and needs. He needs to feel wanted, whether it's indulging him in letting him find his voice in the film or a comforting arm around him when he gets worked up. Attenborough had quickly realised this on *Chaplin* and Gordon followed suit.

'Robert is extremely easy to work with because he's so smart about the material and the character and so communicative that, yes, there's a lot of play and he's coming up with stuff, but as a director that's great. I guess if I was a different kind of director, maybe I wouldn't like it but for me that was wonderful that I could say, "Can we go a little bit more this way?" and he'd do something new and magic would happen. So that's kind of what I want in an actor. I don't want somebody who's just looking to follow orders. I want somebody who's gonna take my limited ideas and make them very alive, and that's what he was really good at so I was very grateful for that.'

Gordon added, 'Robert can take a two-minute scene and take you through five different arcs of emotion as he takes himself through that. Which is very much like life, but not very much like what we usually see in acting. Many actors are more in the tradition of De Niro, where watching the performance is part of the pleasure, being aware that that's the great character that they built. Robert's one of those rare actors who, when you watch him, you go, "Oh, he must just be like that part." And it's only when you see him play fifteen completely different roles that you realise, "Well, wait a minute – he can't be like all these people."

'Robert did thirty-five movies and TV series and he was always fine, a consummate professional. On *Back to School* he was a blast. He was good at hiding [his problem], which is why it went on as long as it did. Now he's completely clean and maybe he's a bit more serious, but he was twenty-three then and he's in his late thirties now.'

The Singing Detective, Gordon said, is about 'a man climbing out from the darkness of his soul and I figured out right away that this could have been about Robert. In the beginning, I think Robert had a hard time acknowledging that, but near the end of filming, I walked up to him and said, "You know what this film is about, don't you?" And he said, "Yes."'

Gibson said about the character, 'The problems we all face, they beat a lot of people. You try and deal with it. You try and manage it. I share that with him.

'I don't know if I've worked with anyone who has as much pure talent as Robert. He's very instinctive. It's an amazing gift. His tremendous talent is part of the reason but it's more than that. There is something so vulnerable, so honest, so sad and so lovable about him. The audience can sense those things, so they keep wanting to see him in movies, and people in the movie industry sense it and keep hiring him. He was a wacky kid, but he's very self-reflective now. He's one of the most lovable people you'll ever meet. You want to mother and father him. He broadcasts a certain amount of innate goodness and he's sweet and vulnerable.'

The movie received a mixed reaction when released at the Sundance film festival, but Robert was in no doubt where he stood. He told the *LA Daily News*, 'I have every reason to be proud of [it]. I won't fight it. I'm proud of how it plays. I'm proud of the people sitting around me when I'm watching it.' The film may not have been a hit, but it proved to the world that he was back in business.

To say congratulations for getting through the film with no real drama, Gibson gave Robert a BMW 650 – to which an astonished Robert replied, 'What are you thinking? To me, that is a serious suicide machine. I take it around once in a while. I am very interested in learning further road safety and, of course, in getting a licence.

'Gibson was always like, "I believe in you, man – you're gonna get through this." And I was like, "Yeah." All that stuff before, where part of the game was the "I promise" – it was all kid's stuff. All "cry wolf" stuff. It wasn't important to me to change. But I'm into this.'

Ironically, it was Robert who had to defend Gibson after the *Lethal Weapon* actor was arrested on 28 July 2006 for a DUI offence. Not only was he doing over 80mph in a 45mph zone – a subsequent breathalyser

Above: In court to hear drug charges in California, 2001.   © *Rex Features*

Below: The role made famous by Michael Gambon in the TV version
of *The Singing Detective* was taken by Downey in the 2003 film with
Mel Gibson.   © *Rex Features*

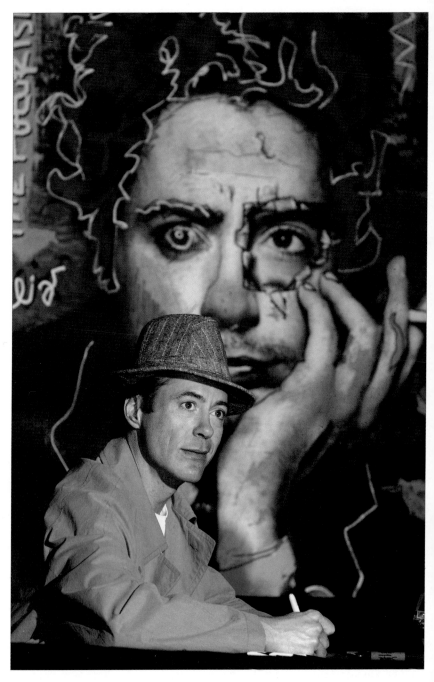

The Futurist was Downey as musician.

Above: Downey plays some songs from *The Futurist*.   © *Rex Features*

Below: Downey with his wife Susan and Indio, the son from his
first marriage.   © *PA Photos*

Above: Downey in a musical interlude with Indio (seated).   © *Rex Features*

Below: In *Good Night and Good Luck* with George Clooney and David Strathairn.   © *Rex Features*

Above: *A Scanner Darkly* featured Downey, Keanu Reeves, Wynona Ryder and Woody Harrelson. The actors were filmed and then the animation was overlayed. © *Rex Features*

Below: Downey had a hit with *Iron Man* in 2008. © *Rex Features*

Above: Hi-jinks in the jungle in *Tropic Thunder*. Jay Baruchel, Brandon T Jackson, Ben Stiller, a blacked-up Downey and Jack Black. © *Rex Features*

Below: Downey with *Sherlock Holmes* director Guy Ritchie and co-star Jude Law with artist and director Sam Taylor-Wood. © *Rex Features*

Above: Downey and Law in *Sherlock Holmes*. © *Rex Features*

Below: Producer Joel Silver was a long-time friend to Downey. © *Rex Features*

Left: Downey won a Golden Globe for *Sherlock Holmes*.

© *Rex Features*

Right: Downey and wife Susan at the 2010 *Vanity Fair* Oscars party.

© *Rex Features*

test showed that he was over the limit – but his anti-Semitic remarks to the arresting police officer James Mee – 'Fucking Jews... Jews are responsible for all the wars in the world' – made it one of the biggest Hollywood scandals in recent years.

Shamed, Gibson was quick to apologise for his drunken remarks, releasing a statement, 'After drinking alcohol on Thursday night, I did a number of things that were very wrong and for which I am ashamed. I drove a car when I should not have and was stopped by the LA County sheriffs. The arresting officer was just doing his job and I feel fortunate that I was apprehended before I caused injury to any other person. I acted like a person completely out of control when I was arrested and said things that I do not believe to be true and which are despicable. I am deeply ashamed of everything I said and I apologise to anyone who I have offended.

'Also, I take this opportunity to apologise to the deputies involved for my belligerent behaviour. They have always been there for me in my community and indeed probably saved me from myself. I disgraced myself and my family with my behaviour and for that I am truly sorry. I have battled the disease of alcoholism for all of my adult life and profoundly regret my horrific relapse. I apologise for any behaviour unbecoming of me in my inebriated state and have already taken necessary steps to ensure my return to health.'

Gibson is also famously said to have asked a female sergeant, 'What are you looking at, sugar tits?' – although it seems increasingly likely that that never happened. Gibson has denied it and it was only reported by an unnamed insider to Hollywood gossip site TMZ.

Gibson entered an out-patient addiction recovery program in a bid to quell the public storm. He also released a second statement, apologising specifically to the Jewish community for his remarks.

Now instead of Robert's friends being asked to comment on yet another setback for him, he was the one being asked to offer his opinion on a friend. He told the media, 'Somebody was being caught in the act of being an imperfect human being. I really didn't know that we had eight million morally sound people in this town. Wow, I really didn't know that. I guess I've been dining at The Ivy with, like, living saints.'

Gibson said, 'He was one of the first people to call and offer the hand of friendship. He just said, "Hey, welcome to the club. Let's go see what we can do to work on ourselves."'

Not that Robert should have been feeling too smug. He was still taking drugs, albeit far less frequently than before. However, a moment of enlightenment was not far away. He was driving his car 'full of tons of fucking dope. I'd already been up for a couple of days and I could have gone on one for the next couple of days. And it probably wouldn't have ended there, were it not for a fast-food meal.

'It was such a disgusting burger I ordered. I had that and this big soda and I thought something really bad was going to happen. I thought I might have a heart attack or have to go to the hospital. So I reached out to some people and said, "I'm really into trouble. I need to curl up for four days and get all this out of my system."'

He then threw all the drugs in the ocean. There was also a stroke of luck for Robert, as days earlier he had been stopped by police. Luckily, they never checked his bag, which was full of drugs. However, he was told that he would have to fix his licence plate.

But the day that he decided to throw the drugs in the ocean would prove to be his epiphany and he never got high again. 'No one ever said, "We need to leave this guy alone for six months or a year, let him go and buy tons of drugs, let him drive around to where all this terrible crap happened and he'll figure it out. No. That'll never work." But for me, that's what did it.

'I never sat in prison and worried about whether I still would have a career when I got out. But I did wonder what I would do next. What do you do when the party's over and you really have to face living your life without drugs?

'I am finding that it's a lot easier to act when you're not tearing yourself up inside. To act is to play an instrument, but how can you play the saxophone when it's filled with Crisco? Right now, all I'm putting into my body are cigarettes and coffee. Those are my last two addictions. And they'll go sooner or later. At this point in my life, I'm going for progress, not perfection.'

Robert's next film was certainly progress, if very little perfection. He would star in *Gothika* – a flimsy B-movie horror film that would see him team up again with his *Weird Science* producer Joel Silver. As Robert has stated, 'I credit [him] with basically reinviting me to the world of big studio movies with *Gothika*.'

Once again, Gibson lent a helping hand, telling Silver (who he was very good friends with) that the 'kid is clean. He's lapsed, but he's a talent that can't be allowed to go to waste.'

Silver gave Robert the script, telling him to read it. Touched, perhaps, to be back in the game, he had no hesitation agreeing to star in the film without actually reading the script. 'And then I read it and I enjoyed it. I really did.'

Silver's leading lady Halle Berry was coming to the film on something of a hot streak, following roles in *Swordfish*, *Monster's Ball* (which she won an Oscar for), *Die Another Day* and the *X-Men* sequel. However, some cynics would say that her next two films – *Gothika* and superhero misfire *Catwoman* – would start her film-career decline.

Gothika sees Berry play a psychiatrist in a women's mental hospital, who suddenly finds herself waking up one day to discover she has been committed to the same mental hospital she works in, accused of murder.

It's competently made and Robert's fans would have been delighted to see him star in a big-budget film again.

Robert would say about the film, 'It's a smart movie, today's version of *The Shining* in an institution and I try to rehabilitate poor, misguided and often violent, sinister women. I'm so much more used to doing something – as James Spader would say – "chewing up the scenery." Or as Tom Sizemore would say, "Making faces for cash and chicken." In this role, I'm doing reacting.'

Director Mathieu Kassovitz said, 'Robert is smart and he has amazing charisma. At the same time, there is an edge to his personality that he put into the character and you really feel it in the film.'

Silver would withhold 40 per cent of Robert's salary against completion of the film to minimise risks. 'We had issues,' he said. 'We had to over-insure – he paid the insurance on *Gothika*, which meant he made no money at the end of it. But in Hollywood, it's simple – if you screw up, they'll kill you. I'd work with him on anything. I'll use him again in a second. I'll try to put him in anything I can.'

It wasn't really a risk for Robert: he had no real choice if he wanted to get back in Hollywood's good books. They'd had their fingers burned once too often with him and he would have to work hard to gain their trust again.

However, he seemed to have enjoyed working on the movie, particularly with Berry. 'When we were working, you wouldn't have known she wasn't crazy. She was really, really down with her method. You have to admire that. It was almost exhausting watching her gear herself up to do what she had to do and it's kind of like watching a great athlete train. You say, "I'd really like to hit the tape and win that race but I wouldn't want to have to get myself into that kind of shape over that space of time." I know what that's like to work like that.

'She was in so many intense scenes and then I'd come in. I don't really approach work all that seriously right up until the moment that I do it and even then, I do a couple of takes and they go, "OK, would you mind coming back in your body and taking this seriously for a minute?" I'm hoping that, occasionally, I offered her some relief to her otherwise very strenuous, exhausting and super-intense role.'

In fact, Berry poured praise and sympathy on Robert. She said, 'I think he is one of this generation's finest actors. He's just one of those people that, no matter how many times he screws up, you have an affinity for him because deep down you know he's a good soul that's struggling with a disease that has him in its grasp. I think everybody wants to always try to give him a chance. He's a good guy. He bought a lot of credibility to the film.'

Robert would say about Berry's thumbs up, 'Hmm... so in case it sucked, it would be my fault too. Why she thought I didn't suck? God, I don't know.'

That was good of her as Berry suffered a nasty accident – breaking her arm – during filming, and naturally Robert was involved. 'It was an accident,' he insisted. 'And I was at fault. She fell on a bed during the scene. She was out for three weeks, but she came back and finished the film in a cast.'

'It wasn't like I was trying to fall fifty feet and fell wrong or did something crazy,' Berry said. "I was doing a scene with Robert and he grabbed my arm the wrong way and broke it.'

Robert added, 'It was bad enough that all the crew were giving me a hard time about beating up a girl. All the girls on set would pretend to be scared when I came near them. They did their best to make me feel embarrassed.'

Director Mathieu Kassovitz said, 'Robert is not a bad guy. He's a true professional, but sometimes difficult. He's a wild actor. He tries to bring something new to each and every scene. Any director would be lucky to have him.'

When the film came out, Robert was delighted to be thrust into the limelight again. 'It's been ages. I have to say that it's really cool at this point. Last night was the *Gothika* premiere here and I was out with my gal and her parents and such and such and all my friends. It was a beautiful situation. People weren't ugly drunk, but it was really happy.'

It seemed his troubled lifestyle was under control, with Robert saying, 'I'm a pretty easy read. I'm either doing well or I'm having a sidebar conversation with the valet at your party and we disappear and come back forty-five minutes later looking very alert. It doesn't interest me at all any more. I'm a lab rat at heart and I miss that "whoopee" feeling, but I've found other ways to get that.

'I'm not in the clear yet. I might be shifting out of my old ways but I'm still the same guy who messed up his life and got into all that trouble. I can be comfortable while someone else enjoys a drink. If I'm out at a restaurant and a waiter asks me if I'd like a glass of wine, I tell him, "I'd love to but I have plans for Christmas." And I'm serious. I don't know whether I miss the euphoria that comes with drinking and drug-taking. But I definitely don't miss what's on the other side of it.'

Talking about what he'd learned about his drug problems, he told *Shortlist*, 'Research complete. All of my data is in – it's a really tough and shitty road to be obsessive about anything. Then again, it's a really huge deal. But if you talk to the leading lights of modern psychiatry, philosophy, anyone who understands human behaviour, they say, "Well, it's perfectly normal for people to have a fixated, obsessive relationship with something for a period of time." And then you know what? It just stops. Just like life. Things go crazy, they get chaotic and the end result is tragic sometimes. But more often than not, people often say, "Oh, that was an incredibly long and mysterious fucked-up phase."'

In 2002, Robert's 2000 drug charges were dismissed and his probation ended after a court determined that he had been substance free for the past 14 months. Following the court ruling, his lawyer, Jim Epstein, said that his client was 'absolutely ecstatic and very optimistic he'll be able to stay sober and get movie parts again'.

A constant factor in Robert getting – and staying – clean is the helping hand of *Gothika* producer, Susan Levin. As Robert said, '[*Gothika*] is special for us in more ways than one. We met on it, we're in love and engaged and all that fun stuff.'

A rising film producer, Levin – like Sarah Jessica Parker – was the complete opposite of Robert. Where he is a bundle of nervous energy, she is composed. However, Susan insists she didn't even find him attractive when they first met. 'Not even a little bit,' she told *Harpers Bazaar*. 'The main thing I remember about meeting him was thinking how strange he was. I thought he was a brilliant actor, but it didn't go beyond that. I saw him more like a professor or someone's older brother.

'Four of us would work out together after the shoot and one day, when we were on the treadmills, Robert goes, "Levin, you wanna go to dinner?" and I said, "Eh, I'll grab something to eat," so we agreed to go change and meet in the lobby. And as he walked down the stairs toward me, I remember looking up at him and suddenly thinking, "He's really cute."'

She went on to add, 'He wasn't someone I was considering, you know, getting together with, so it wasn't that I had to be leery. I was more like, "OK, is he going to show up for the day?" You know, it wasn't about anything beyond that. And then it kind of evolved and a relationship started forming, but he didn't really ask me out.

'We were on location, and so you're like, "Is there going to be life after this?" I mean, he's an actor. I have a real job. I'm in the office every day, you know, or I'm on location or something, so I figured it was kind of fun and it kept us occupied in Montreal and stuff like that. But he didn't really ask me out. What happened was, we had all gone away for Easter. And at one point, we're in the room together by ourselves and he turns to me and he goes, "So you want to make out?" And I was like, "No."'

'She meant it too,' Downey would add. 'I was like, "Wow, she's not kidding. That's a real no."'

Susan is now unofficially known as the miracle that saved Robert Downey Jr. 'I was never a partier,' she said. 'I used to enjoy some red wine, but now I don't do anything. I don't have a history of making bad choices. And if my parents had any reservations – whether they were scared about [his being] an actor or an addict or that he'd gone to prison or had a kid and an ex-wife: the whole shebang of things I claimed I would never want in a guy and add some new things to it – they never shared them with me. They saw how happy I was.

'There can only be one rock star in our relationship and I'm fine with that. I've always been someone who would rather have someone compliment me when I'm out of the room than to my face, whereas Robert is the opposite. So I'm happy to support him.'

The stable family lifestyle didn't come easy for Robert, as Susan said about their early days: 'He'd be driving home and I'd say, "Drive safely." He'd be like, "What do you mean? Do you think I'm not a good driver?" "No, dude, that's what you say when you care about someone."'

'I met the right gal,' Robert said. 'She's very direct and straightforward. I think that relationship has been very settling and very profound. It is me being comfortable in my skin.'

Robert proposed to Susan in London on 6 November, a minute before the end of her birthday. 'She only said she'd accept my proposal of marriage as long as I promised to stay sober and drug free. "I'm not doing that dance with you. I'm drawing a line in the sand here." She was absolutely clear about it. That doesn't mean that other women, business associates, movie directors, insurance companies, judges and law enforcement hadn't been clear about it too.'

They would marry in 2005 at a private home in the Hamptons. To calm his nerves he had a 30-minute kung-fu session shortly before the ceremony.

He said, 'She will be Mrs Downey for the rest of her days on earth if I have anything to say about it. My wedding ring means everything to me. I had it inscribed with the Latin for "Until the wheels fall off" and I mean that.'

Of Indio Susan said, 'With step-kids, it's hard at first. But, like anything, my approach was to just be honest about it and not try and force anything – not act like we were a big family right away. What's come from that is a really great relationship with Indio, because I didn't try to make it into something it wasn't … until one day, it was.'

Robert added, 'My son guides me. That's why I was recently out at a quarter to midnight stalking David Beckham, because that little prick wanted a picture.'

Times were still tight for Robert. Money from *Gothika* and his next movie *Kiss Kiss Bang Bang* was going straight on to pay his debts. In 2003 it was reported he might be filing for bankruptcy very soon. He didn't even have a place of his own – he was living rent free in a 'ratty old ranch house' in Malibu, owned by soundtrack composer and producer Jonathan Elias.

'We have an apartment, which is a little bigger than a hotel room,' Robert said. 'She has her scripts everywhere and we have this massage table in the middle of the room. We step over each other, saying, "Whose towel is this?" and sometimes I find my socks in her purse. It's ridiculous. Sometimes she calms me down and other times she's the reason I'm annoyed.'

But as this was the reformed hellraiser's second marriage, he admitted it was still early days. 'We're still getting to know each other – but every couple goes on that voyage of discovery. If I leave the house with my hair washed and my shoes on the right feet, then these days I'm in good shape.

'I am not used to being happy, because I was really busy either working or getting stoned for the past fourteen years. I probably should meditate for four years with meal breaks. Susan understands that she'll probably live another four years with me in hell before we'll be happy. But she gets it: I am a work in progress.'

Susan added, 'He's completely eccentric but grounded. He's someone who has lived so much life yet has almost a Peter Pan kind of never-grow-up quality.'

Conceding that he still has a drama-queen element in him – to the point that he tends 'to bring out the co-dependent element in anyone I'm in close proximity to' – Robert admitted that his friends still worried about him.

'It's Team Downey. But it's Team Esoterica – kung fu, therapy. It's like I am surrounded like an MIT prodigy with teams and squads of experts and supporters. Some of it's some real grassroots shit, but it's that thing of, how much support do you need? What kind and for how long?

'Sure I have turned my life around, but I will also never forget that time I was in the gutter. It's important for me that I often remind myself of that, so that it never happens again. But yes, I am now a respectable married man.

'I am clean, I work, I am in love. It is almost like a perfectly normal life. I have stability now. Of course, I am afraid of falling back into the clutches of substance abuse – everybody is – but my wife is there for me. I have made mistakes in the past, but they are now a part of me. I can only look ahead and hope that I now do better.'

Under his wife's guidance, Robert would try and think more long-term about his film career. 'My wife tells me that my mission, if I should choose to accept it, is to get in and stay within the mainstream and then deviate to do things that are of interest to me. I have been around for ages. I have never been the lead in a big hit movie. There's all kinds of experiences that I haven't had that many of my peers have had and take for granted – just like I took things for granted in the past and paid for it dearly.

'The truth of the matter is that at this point I have nothing to prove: the experiences now are ways of being able to feel a sense of fulfilment, which I wasn't allowing myself to feel before.'

Robert's next step was to team up with producer Joel Silver once more in the vastly underrated *Kiss Kiss Bang Bang*. A comedy crime thriller (and noir send-up), it tells the story of Harry, a small-time thief who accidentally joins a movie audition to play a detective and becomes involved in a murder investigation.

Robert had his wife to thank for even knowing about the script. 'I saw her reading this script and she was laughing her ass off,' he remembered. 'I asked what it was and she said, "It's just this Johnny Knoxville project – don't worry about it." I asked what was so funny and she said that in the script a dog just took this guy's severed finger out of an ice bowl. I asked why his finger was in an ice bowl. And she said it was cut off by his girlfriend. I said, "If he got it cut off by his girlfriend, why did he put it in an ice bowl? Why didn't he just go to hospital?" She said, "He did and then it got pulled off by these guys." What guys? "Oh Mr Frying Pan and Mr Fire." Who are they? And she goes, "It's a long story but it's a really good script."'

Intrigued, Robert soon discovered that she was correct in her assessment of *Kiss Kiss Bang Bang*. It was a script Robert loved desperately, even saying that it might be his favourite role of all time. 'I love the scene where Harry turns up at a pool party and gets to chat to this girl who asks him what he does and he goes, "I invented dice when I was a kid. Now I'm retired." I was always kind of full of shit. I went from New York to LA just like Harry and when I arrived there I remember telling people the reason I moved was I'd been working for the Irish mafia and some bad stuff had gone down and I had to get out of town. Just shit.'

He also knew this was a film he couldn't let slip past him. 'It's like fate or circumstance or whatever it is – I guess I was just meant to do it,' he said.

Robert wasn't first choice for Harry, with Colin Farrell reported to be the studio's favoured option. Writer Shane Black – whose first directing role this was – also revealed that he was under pressure to cast actors like Harrison Ford, but said, 'As Robert read the lines, I felt like I'd typed them right into his mouth.'

'I wondered which A-list actor was going to get the role instead of me,' sighed Downey. He also said, 'I'm probably the best deal in town, literally bargain basement. Right now all these guys you've never heard of are making $8 million a movie, so I'm still a good deal.'

When Black followed his instincts and cast Robert as Harry, producer Joel Silver backed him up. 'There's something about Harry (Robert's character) that keeps you rooting for him, despite his tendency to get in his own way. We needed an actor who could convey the character's blend of optimism, recklessness, misguided persistence and likeability. In addition to his obvious talents as an actor, Robert exudes a boyish charm and an appeal that is perfect for Harry.'

However, another of the film's producers, Carrie Morrow, admitted that Robert was under constant scrutiny from the cast and crew over fears he would relapse. While insurance was a tetchy point for Robert, it was with *Kiss Kiss Bang Bang* that studio bosses were 'just starting to trust him' according to Morrow. 'They were willing to let the rope out enough to see if he would fall. And he didn't. He was punctual. He was professional. He was respectable.'

Problems with insurance had meant that Robert had failed to land a starring role in Woody Allen's *Melinda and Melinda* a year earlier. Allen, who also failed to cast Wynona Ryder because of the same issues, said, 'The completion bonding companies would not bond the picture unless we could insure them. We were heartbroken because I had worked with Wynona Ryder before and thought she was perfect for this, and wanted to work with Bob Downey and always thought he was a huge talent.'

Robert, however, was quoted by the *New York Times* as saying, 'I get my hands on [Woody Allen], I'm going to catch another felony case. The reality was I didn't even want the part. They should have looked into the insurance issue first. I'm happy to be out of it. It makes me look as if I am unemployable, yet I've finished two films with no problems. For *Gothika*, the insurance thing was settled before filming began. They took forty cents out of every dollar I was paid and, when the movie was finished, they gave some of it back to me. Fine. Whatever. Whatever is necessary.'

Kiss Kiss Bang Bang was Shane Black's directorial debut. He had carved a career out of writing darkly humorous thrillers like the first two *Lethal Weapon* movies and *The Last Boy Scout*, but he was desperate to try his hand at directing. Eyebrows were raised, however, when he cast his two leading men. Not only had he hired Robert but he had employed Val Kilmer as well. Hiring these two could be a stressful job for a seasoned professional, never mind a beginner. Robert's personal troubles we all know about, while Kilmer was once described as 'one of the scariest people in Hollywood'. *Tombstone* screenwriter Kevin Jarre said, 'There's a dark side to Val that I don't feel comfortable talking about.'

The making of *The Island of Dr Moreau* is one of the legendary nightmare tales of movie making. A major reason for that was the casting of Marlon Brando and Kilmer, with the director, John Frankenheimer, saying as Kilmer finished his last scene, 'Cut! Now get that bastard off my set.' Later he would add for good measure, 'I will never climb Mount Everest and I will never work with Val Kilmer again!'

Undeterred, Black presided over *Kiss Kiss Bang Bang* with a calm and easygoing touch. Much like *True Believer*, it was a fun, playful set for Robert and, like James Woods on that film, Val Kilmer proved something of an equal to Robert.

Black said, 'It's one of those fortunate pairings. The star of the movie is the fact that these two guys are together. How could you not love that? You don't know what you're buying, but you know something great is going to happen. They've never been in a movie [together] before and I thought, "Who knows what's going to happen when you take Robert Downey Jr, with all his volatility, and Val, with his ... well ... volatility, and when you throw them together?

Something's going to happen." So to me, the star of the film is this incredible coming together.'

Robert would later joke that Black was using his name to drum up free publicity before the film's release.

At the start Kilmer, however, was unconvinced about working with Black. 'We sat down in meetings. You know he's a first-time director, you can't have a conversation about directing really. There's no way to interview someone about it. Joel [Silver] said, "I hired him, he's good, don't worry." And that was it. "Trust me, he's great." And as soon as Joel said that, I knew that Joel doesn't really make mistakes. He's one of the top five guys, right? He was very, very happy.

'Also, I think it's a tribute to him – seriously – about the riskier or stranger comedy bits in it that Joel just liked and he trusted Shane. Joel just said to Warner Bros, "What will it take to leave me alone?" and that money, whatever that was, was what we had to work with.'

'I think that Val wanted to do something funny,' Black remembered. 'He wanted to do a comedy. He kept saying, "Don't people remember that I did *Real Genius*? You know, I did *Top Secret*. I'm funny." I said, "OK, we know, we know."

'There's some performers you know what you're buying. You get the performance you pay for. With those two guys, I had no idea what we were going to get. I just knew that, whatever it was, it was going to be something that you just wanted to look at. It was going to be amazing.'

Kilmer added of Black, 'He is very calm. I probably went to Robert immediately when I saw it was calm bordering on comatose. I thought, "Well, he's deer in the headlights, he's frozen, we're in trouble." It was simply that he was so well prepared and he never changed really. He never raised his voice once. And it's a frustrating job.'

'I love actors,' Black said. 'I mean, what concerns them concerns me. I think I get it a little bit, you know? And when people were expressing concerns about Kilmer and Downey in the same movie. I'm a first-time director – you know, what's my ability to deal with these two vivid personalities? But look, we got the bargain of the century. These guys came to me, they cut their price. They did this movie for me. This is luck you get once in a lifetime.'

Kilmer and Robert had met years before at the MTV awards, but Robert had thought Kilmer was standoffish. However, they would bond like old pals on the film.

'We thought it was there,' remembered Robert. 'But we didn't know it worked until the first day of shooting. We would say, "Oh my God, if we're goofing around on the sidelines and it's funny, and we just walk in front of the camera and start doing the script and it works, that would be really cool." It's great because you don't have to worry about yourself when you're concentrating on your repartee with someone else. And it so seldom happens. You're almost in a fucking vacuum doing your part in a scene with people you like, dislike or are indifferent toward. And then they do their side and you try and show up and be the good off-camera actor and then they swing the lens around and you suddenly get a little more self-conscious and you're wondering, "Are *they* going to give *me* their all?" This was never like that. We fucked with each other for six weeks and they filmed it. That's essentially what happened.'

Kilmer in turn raved about Robert. 'I always like a good laugh and Robert's very, very funny. One of my favourite things about Robert is his observations. The things he sees in people and their characters are invariably interesting and entertaining. And he usually says it in an interesting way.

'Robert is so fast, it's absurd. I don't know if it's because of his past addictions, but I know he hasn't begun to show us what he can do because he was so high for these past performances. With this, we just went to the core.'

Talking about his kissing scene with Kilmer, Robert joked, 'Well, his lips are pretty famous and I could name three dozen women who could tell you what it's like kissing them. But I wanted to find out for myself.'

'Everybody was watching him,' Kilmer said. 'Everybody was waiting for the other shoe to drop. The funny thing about Robert is that he has awkward mannerisms to begin with. He's kind of a quirky dude. People assumed he was wasted even when he was sober.

I actually had somebody come up to me and say, "I'm sure he's wasted. He's out of his mind." It was projected onto him, almost like he couldn't escape it.'

Robert would spend his time on set learning kung fu: 'Everyone would break for lunch and I would have my kung-fu guy come by and we would train on the set. He would ask what scene we were training for and I'd say it was just for me and the next grade of belt. Right now I am in the medium blue-sash grade – it's about halfway to black belt.

'What I can do now is defend myself against practically anybody as opposed to hurting someone – I don't want to do that. I wanted to do something that was martial arts but that wasn't angry because I'm angry enough as it is. It has been great though, it has done wonders.'

Robert would also be involved with power-flow yoga from his teacher Vinnie Marino, who was part of the Team Downey support group. 'I need a lot of support, like Lance Armstrong,' Robert told *Time* magazine. 'Life is really hard and I don't see some active benevolent force out there. I see it as basically a really cool survival game. You get on the right side of the tracks and you now are actually working with what some people would call magic. It's not. It's just you're not in the fucking dark any more, so you know how to get along a little better, you know?'

Kiss Kiss Bang Bang was a classic Downey Jr performance – a frantic livewire jack-in-the-box. But if

Robert had hoped to escape his past, he found he couldn't when it came to promoting the film. In a press conference for the movie – and in front of foreign writers – a woman journalist asked, 'Could you describe what it was like to go through recovery?'

A visibly frustrated Robert said that he no longer wanted to talk about his past indiscretions.

'Then I have nothing,' the woman said, clearly annoyed.

There were, however, certain occasions when he would relent. 'As a rule, I don't like to talk about it,' he said, 'but if I'm really tired or really bored or we can't get on to a more interesting subject, I'll talk about it.'

He certainly couldn't avoid the topic when he went on the Oprah Winfrey show. 'When I met with her producers, I said, "Do we really have to dredge all this up again? It's been discussed endlessly." And they said, "Yes, but not to Oprah."'

Sadly, the film would flop at the box office, but it was a huge hit with the critics. The Portland *Oregonian* observed that, 'This is one of Downey's most enjoyable performances and one of Kilmer's funniest. It's a relationship comedy wrapped in sharp talk and gunplay, a triumphant comeback for Black and one of the year's best movies.'

Talking about the box-office disappointment, Robert said, 'I'm fine. Look – disappointment, humility, it's all part of the same thing. I look for the highest degree of difficulty and disappointment – it just becomes better quality. Like I said, life's really messy. But again, either the cosmos has order to it or it doesn't and I chose to believe it does. So to judge or to compare is a really dangerous pastime.

'I think I hold the record for being the actor who had done the most movies and [to] still be getting paid the same amount I was three movies in. "How much is so and so making?" "He's making four million dollars." "What's his name again?" "Well, he was in this movie and it wasn't a hit but, boy is he hot." "Wow, how the fuck did he do that?" It's my lot in life to be patient and wait and be disappointed because it's not about your day job anyway. It's about what you're here to do. Whatever that is.'

Robert's next lot in life was to raise a few eyebrows when he agreed to star alongside Tim Allen in Disney's family comedy *The Shaggy Dog*.

'I just wanted to be in a Disney movie and they offered it. Best job I ever had. The craft service is amazing. Fucking crazy. "Hey, thanks, we got that shot with you and the monkeys, we'll see you in three weeks, did you get your cheque?" I'm like, "Wow!"

'I think it's pretty clear that if you do a bunch of movies back to back and you're not struggling to be responsible, you know that a certain phase is complete. I think Disney hiring me is a good indication of that. It's weird. It hasn't been that long. It's just that you can tell when someone's changed, just as you can tell when they're behaving as though they've changed but nothing's different.'

During the making of the film, a crewmember on the set approached his him, saying he had known Robert as a child. 'He came up to me and said, "I used to babysit you when your dad was making *Pound*. I know what it was like back then." And he handed me the slate from *Pound*, which was the first movie I was ever in and it said "3/17/70". So it was literally like thirty-five years ago and change.

'It looked like something the art department had come up with to look like a period collector's item, like Sotheby's. So lately there's been a whole sense of closure.'

He later said, 'I may have shot myself in the foot but, creatively, I still have a good reputation.' – and he would prove that by starring in 2005's *Good Night and Good Luck*, which was directed by George Clooney. The film told the true story of journalist Edward Murrow's fight against right-wing Senator Joseph McCarthy, who led the notorious witch hunt against people suspected of being communist sympathisers in America in the 1950s. The movie also boasted an impressive cast, full of hugely talented actors like David Strathairn, Ray Wise, Patricia Clarkson, Frank Langella and Jeff Daniels, as well as Clooney himself.

Good Night and Good Luck saw Robert play a much more understated character than normal, leaving him to comment, 'It was tough for me to play a guy who's essentially very simple and dedicated and communicative. He didn't have a bunch of tag lines, he wasn't very dramatic – just basically a normal, happy, hard-working guy. Kinda like me now.'

He added about the film, 'I was tired and stressed and had stopped smoking, but the whole fabulous boys club aside, George Clooney really rolls up his sleeves and knows how to direct.'

Strangely, the normally liberal actor added, 'I don't agree with the politics of *Good Night and Good Luck*. Let me put it this way: they touch on some really important stuff. But sometimes, these witch hunts and these fear things come from people who know very, very well that the public may always scream for its constitutional whatever, but that they are in danger. And they are in danger from a very formidable enemy. This is the same way I felt after I went and did time. This is crazy for me to say, but there really isn't all that much to rehabilitating people. There is containing things and enforcing harm-reduction to the public and all that. But, essentially, people are really stubborn.

'I'm a little more right wing than I used to be, that's all. But I don't want to be political.'

Next Robert would star in *A Scanner Darkly* – with director Richard Linklater luring in several other A-list actors, including Keanu Reeves, Woody Harrelson and Winona Ryder. Because of the movie's animation presentation of a science-fiction story, the attraction was that there would be no make-up sessions, endless costume changes or constant delays because of lighting a shot, etc.

'There is kind of an animation ghetto that exists in the industry,' Linklater said. 'From the beginning, we lived with the Hollywood truism that adults don't see animated movies. But I have always had the response that, yeah, adults don't go see animated movies – until they do! All it takes is one movie.'

Talking about the film, Robert said, 'I thought it was probably the strangest script I ever read. But I knew Keanu was doing it and the director was Richard Linklater and I thought, "These guys are pretty smart and know a good role." I really loved my character too. He reminds me of those propellerhead guys that you knew in high school who knew how to take apart a bike and put it back together and other freaky stuff. I thought it would be really fun to play him.'

The film also saw Robert choose the quality of the script over the pay packet. 'At a certain point you have to think, how much more of your life do you want to enjoy and how much are you sacrificing by how much harder you have to work... So now I tend to look at things as like, "Am I going to be stronger, wiser and gladder if I shoot a certain movie?" It becomes a bit more of an intuitive game.'

A Scanner Darkly is about an undercover cop who becomes involved with a dangerous new drug and begins to lose his identity. Robert said about the film's themes, 'Paranoia goes from generation to generation.

It's convenient if you're neurotic to imagine that there're a few people controlling everything. That way it's manageable and small – like asking the Wizard of Oz to tell you the truth. But that's not life – life is messy.'

He admitted, however, he saw similarities with his own situation. 'It wasn't a cathartic or luminous thing for me because the movie is about a drug-addled society. Watching the movie, it was kind of funny how my character's paranoid can-I-trust-my-buddies references were so sick and so fun to see.'

It was a six-week shoot – and one that featured a sort of summer-camp atmosphere thanks to the joviality and on-set improv work form Robert and Harrelson. Reeves' manager, Erwin Stoff, told *Wired*, 'It was a socialist endeavour of sorts. We all gathered at the Four Seasons and rehearsed, shot and worked on the script. There were no image issues. It was all about being true to the characters, which is a rare thing to have.'

To cope with saying a thousand words of dialogue per day, Robert came up with an unusual technique. 'I take all the words and then I take the first letter of each word and then I write that out as a long acronym and put it on a poster. Then I'll look at it in the corner of the room instead of watching TV after I'm done working... and then I'll just study it so it just kinda looks like one long weird thing. It is now a study technique that I originated.'

However, the slow progress of the Rotoscoping technique – in which animators trace over live action footage – posed difficulties for Linklater, despite having used it for *Waking Life* five years earlier. He would leave the team of animators to work on the movie while he went on to shoot the remake of *Bad News Bears*, but the work wasn't being done quickly enough and the film's bosses – Warner Independent Pictures – were getting nervous.

After *Bad News Bears* was finished, Linklater then starting work on *Fast Food Nation*, while still waiting for the animation process to finish. Towards the end of the 15th month of animation, he explained, 'I go crazy because it feels like the animation process just goes too slow. I would look over the shoulder of an animator one week and then look a week later and it felt like very little had gone on. So just to keep myself sane I like to work on other things.'

Unfortunately, the finished film was a flawed but sporadically interesting and inventive film. It seemed to escape cinemagoers, but with the delay in the animation constantly pushing the schedule back, there wasn't enough time to market it. President of Warner Independent, Mark Gill, said, 'There's a million pieces that come from a finished film that you need for advertising. Quite frankly, we were running up against too tight a deadline. This is all new to me. It's animation with first-of-its-kind technology and there are challenges that come with that. Our hope is that we will be the first smart movie of the summer.'

That never happened, but Robert was on something

of a roll in playing interesting characters and starring in interesting films. 'Years ago people would say to me, "I think your best work is ahead of you," and I used to think, "Have they seen *Chaplin*? How dare they talk to me like that," but they were right. I'm really enjoying my work right now. If this is a part of my story – and it is a story – when we are dealing with someone who has been around as long as I have and put themselves and their public at large through all these rollercoaster moments, then this is the part of the story when I have my comeback.'

Robert would keep that momentum going by signing on for David Fincher's *Zodiac*, a retelling of the famous San Francisco serial-murder case. Fincher would call Robert 'one of our beloved talents', while Jake Gyllenhaal was so excited to hear about him being cast that he said, 'I knew it was going to be a master class.'

Based on the book of the same name by Robert Graysmith, Fincher's ambitious film would be an incredibly thorough look at the complications, the hindrances and the personal toll that an attempt to stop a serial killer would take on a group of characters.

Robert would play journalist Paul Avery, with Fincher reasoning, 'If a character is going to disappear halfway through the film, you give it to the actor who's going to leave a mark. So people will miss him when he's gone. Paul Avery is the most mercurial character in the movie and I knew Downey would just kill him.'

He added that the role of the hard-drinking Avery

was perfect for Robert 'because he knows how to grasp those inner demons'.

'I'm not so sure that's a compliment,' said Robert, before adding, 'No – I get it, but seriously, drink and drugs are just not part of my life any more, so anything that I achieve on screen, the process is just a technical endeavour.'

'Downey couldn't look less like Paul Avery,' said Fincher. 'I look more like Avery than Downey does. But Downey has the essence that he thought Avery would be like. Those were those kind of guys who maybe drunk a little too much. They were characters. They were guys who for the most part lived on the sidelines of what was going on, but they had incredible grandiose self-images and saw themselves as part of the story.'

Fincher's on-set perfectionism is legendary, as Robert found out. 'In an ideal world, I'd like to do one take of a scene and spend the rest of the day reading newspapers. No animals were hurt in the making of *Zodiac*, but that's where the humane behaviour ended. No ego was left untarnished. There's not much ego left when you're on your fortieth take and Fincher says, "Everything that Downey has just spent the last six hours doing? Let's delete that, go to lunch and start over." There were times when I took it from him and times when I didn't.'

Fincher's insistence on multiple takes would also annoy Jake Gyllenhaal. However, the director defended his process, saying, 'If an actor is going to let the role come to them, they can't resent the fact that I'm willing to wait as long as that takes. You know, the first day of production in San Francisco we shot fifty-six takes of Mark and Jake – and it's the fifty-sixth take that's in the movie.'

But Robert's upward turn in his work life – 'It's different now because it's fun to show up on set' – was also spreading into his personal life, particularly with his son. 'I'm more responsible now,' he said. 'While I can't imagine ever turning into a wrathful father, I let him know there's a price for stepping out of the parameters. I'm willing to be the square dad if that means imposing a few hard edges from time to time. I have no urge to be my kid's best friend. I've been that boy and it feels creepy to think about.

'Yesterday I'd made an appointment at four o'clock for Indio to get a haircut. He doesn't want to do it. I know he doesn't like sitting in a chair for forty-five minutes having his hair cut, but he's going to do it. Why does it matter? Because there's a lesson in delayed gratification that needs to be instituted here and I'm the guy for the job. We've got an appointment and we're going to goddamn keep it. It is not about how Indio feels or what he wants to do. It is that he is going to be glad he did it, even though he can't see that right now. I can see what he cannot see.

'What I want for my son is for him to be honest and happy.'

While work was coming in at a steady rate, Robert

conceded that they weren't 'breathtaking epics'. Deciding to put his energy elsewhere for a while, he decided to write an album of music. He told the *New York Times*, 'Clearly, I have some hesitation in being an actor who puts out an album. But after years of writing songs, it gradually became more real. Then after I got a record deal – and strangely the guy who was heading it up at Sony, Peter Gelb, was not a sleazebag – I couldn't stop it once I said, "Where's my advance money?"'

Music had played an important part in Robert's life from a young age. 'When I was twelve, we were living in Woodstock, there was a piano in the living room. Mom and Dad were breaking up, it was there, I went over. I learned a simple scale and then I realised I could play and I escaped in that. I associate music with a healthy escapism. I was reading Plato, I think, when he was talking about this perfect society. Basically, he said, "Master the body and add music." And I think that's true.

'I think that music can help master the body too. I don't know that music has been recognised for what it really is. It was communicated to me very clearly that music was something well beyond what I was listening to on the record player or on the radio. It was something that transcended all mediums and could interact with a variety of different experiences. With great alacrity it could do anything.

'Living in Greenwich Village in a loft with my mom, dad and my sister, I remember seeing a TV commercial saying "Keep New York City Clean" and I was really engaged by how cool the piano lick sounded. When my dad was writing, he'd play Coltrane and Mingus and Art Pepper and Jefferson Starship and Aretha Franklin. But he would just put an album on repeat. We'd hear *Let it Bleed* literally fifteen to twenty times a day. Lemme tell you, that really seeps in when you're a kid.

'At that point I was introverted. On my own one day, I went to the piano in the corner and started playing that "Keep New York City Clean" commercial.'

Whenever Robert plays music, he admits that it reminds him of his mother. 'I just remember her sitting at the piano and making stuff up – hers is more like smoky lounge than mine. I don't think I've heard my father sing once. I just think we're extensions of our parents' qualities for better or for worse.

'I know that I like writing music. I partnered up with a guy, [composer] Jonathan Elias, who's just leaving the music industry and wants to get into film. But we've been writing music together for some years now. But you think that it's hard to get a film done, with a schedule? Imagine finishing a couple of albums and a musical revue and a bunch of music with no schedule.

'It's a major fricking undertaking. I'm used to coming to work and the call sheet saying, "seven am, scene fourteen b, this costume." Then they say, "Action!" until you're done. The autonomy and self-agency necessary to do a record were new to me. It felt more like the responsibility of being a director who is also in his own movie. Then I figured if people didn't like it, I could always use another dose of humility. Instead, people were pleasantly surprised it didn't suck.

'Nothing is more boring than acting, because as an actor you never have to be proactive about scheduling,' he added. 'You get the call sheet – "Here we have to do this scene today." This was more like – "There are seventeen different songs you can choose for this album. Finish them."'

Sony's Peter Gelb said, 'Robert is a brilliantly gifted songwriter who writes lyrics that are wise and moving. His burnished, smoky voice is an expressive and touching medium for the songs that he has written.'

Robert was quick to point out that he was under no illusion that the reason he was given a record contract was because of who he was and what he'd done. 'Look, it's not like I'm pushing schlock, but nowhere on God's green earth would I be a new recording artist who would be getting on *Oprah* without *Weird Science* and the penitentiary. It's the perfect combination, pretty divine. But it's a gross-out too. Beyond nepotism. No way would I ever get to express myself musically if I wasn't an actor of ill repute. You don't get on *Oprah* if you leave a gleaming life and then just happen to cross over into music. So yeah, I'm a little bit uncomfortable about it.

'I recorded the album with some friends and it just all seemed quite natural. Some of the songs sound more produced than others, but I'm happy with it. Was I worried that people would read too much into the lyrics? Well, that would be my inclination with any record that I hear. Some of the lyrics might have originated from a period of heartbreak, but when I actually wrote songs like "Broken" and "Details", it's really more about characters. I'm not quite narcissistic enough to think people would be dying to hear songs about me.'

On its release in 2004, *The Futurist* – which also included a duet with Jon Anderson on Yes's classic "Your Move" and concluded with a jazz-trio interpretation of Charlie Chaplin's 'Smile' in Robert's throaty croon – received decidedly mixed reviews. The *Scotsman* praised the musical compositions but added that it has 'some of the worst lyrical atrocities ever committed'. Boston College magazine the *Heights* said it 'was partly laudable, partly laughable', while MSN claimed it was 'unpredictably moving'.

After the album flopped, Robert said, 'I don't see why I'd want to do another album. *The Futurist* came out and made its money back, but I worked my ass off and I was not compensated in the fashion I was accustomed to.

'I adore music,' he added. 'Though the album I made didn't really get the support from my label, but then if I was a label and I looked at what I'd got – Destiny's Child or the guy from *Ally McBeal* – then OK, fair point. But I've got no intentions of giving it up.'

His singing career might have stalled, but his acting career was about to be given a mainstream boost.

15

ROBERT STEELS HIMSELF FOR FUTUE SUCCESS

*'I imagined myself playing [a superhero] every
year. They just never gave me the part'*
ROBERT DOWNEY JR

In a way Robert was always destined to be part of the summer-blockbuster crowd. His parents' idea of making something for a larger audience would have been shooting in colour, but when asked if he would prefer a box-office smash or an award, Robert immediately opted for the box-office smash. He loves crowd-pleasing fare – revels in the fun if done right. And even then, it doesn't even have to be done right. 'I can go see a pretty crappy movie and love it, if it's got a couple of things that work. I'm like a soccer coach with kids who shouldn't be playing soccer.'

However, while Robert felt he was perfect for the role of Iron Man ('I love Marvel comics and I grew up reading *Iron Man* and *Spider-Man*'), the chances of him playing Tony Stark were minimal to say the least. While he had impressed in his recent films and his personal problems seemed to be in the past, this was a summer blockbuster with hopes of spawning a franchise. It was unlikely that a studio would grant a multiple-picture deal to an actor who has had as many problems as Robert.

So when his name was talked about in a conversation between director Jon Favreau and producer Kevin Feige, both thought he would be an interesting choice but quickly dismissed it as being potentially risky. However, the idea lingered in their heads. A call to insurance companies showed that he was no longer a risk and the pair talked to former colleagues to see what he was like. They even used his casting in *The Shaggy Dog* to prove that he wasn't a risk to Disney, so why should he be to them?

Another story was that they were told that 'under no circumstances are we [Marvel Studios] prepared to hire him for any price'.

Favreau told a dejected Robert, 'Look – I fought, I tried, I did what I could. It's a pity and a shame, but unfortunately it's going to stop here.'

Robert said, 'With your permission, I'm going to hold out hope.'

It was that sense of optimism that persuaded Favreau to try again.

Robert was so desperate to star in the film, he was willing to screen test for the role – something, bar *Chaplin*, he had not done for a long, long time.

'He really, really wanted it,' said Susan. 'Other than Chaplin, it's the role he's gone after the hardest. He knew he could do it and he knew he had to prove it to people.'

Talking about Robert's audition, Feige remembered, 'A lot of it was in the script and it sounds like he's riffing. A lot of it was riffed. Most of it was "branched out".'

"If you're going to spend a hundred million bucks on a movie, why not see who works?' said Robert.

Once the studio bosses saw Robert's screen test it became quickly apparent that he was the perfect choice to play Tony Stark.

Announcing the news to the world, Feige said, 'Robert Downey Jr is one of the most talented and acclaimed actors of this generation. His versatility sets him apart and makes him an ideal fit to play such a complex character as Iron Man. We could not think of another actor better suited to bring one of Marvel's crown jewels to the big screen and be the centrepiece of our first independently produced feature.'

Favreau quickly saw how revitalised Robert was on set. Hoping that Robert could imprint himself on the role with quirky mainstream appeal as Christian Bale had on *Batman* and Johnny Depp on *Pirates of the Caribbean*, Favreau said, 'Downey wasn't the most obvious choice, but he understood what makes the character tick. He found a lot of his own life experiences in Tony Stark.

'He's somebody who's had it, lost it and now has it again, and it's like a pit bull who's got his jaws on a chew toy. Nothing will take this away from him again,' said Favreau. 'Nobody went to see a movie about the pirate ride at Disneyland. They got interested in it because of Johnny Depp. When Robert was cast in *Iron Man*, it was as if a weight had been lifted off my shoulders. He was not the obvious choice, but my larger fear was making a mediocre movie: the landscape of the superhero is very picked over. I knew that Robert's performance would elevate the movie.'

'Tony Stark offered me the chance of a lifetime,' Robert said simply, adding, 'I have fucking nerd-gasms about this type of stuff.'

Talking about his shape, he said, 'The physical part was I had been, for some reason or another, training for a couple of months before and I'd been in martial arts for five years now. I was kind of up to speed, but wasn't. I figured if I was going to try to look like I was in shape, I might as well do it before I was too old to have it be feasible or matter. And it was a physically demanding part, so the training really helped a lot. Sometimes you just train just to be able to survive what you're going to have to do on the job.'

It was more than a decade since Robert had been in his 20s, and he would have to get fit. 'I'm not twenty-eight or some guy like Daniel Craig who's already got meat packed on his shoulders and they just swelled them up for that,' he said. 'You've seen me in all the movies. I'm not like Mr Buff Guy and now I'm in the over-forty crew, so it has literally been this excruciating process of working out so hard and so often just to not look like a pot-bellied pig.

'Yoga and eating right and all the supplements and sleeping right and all the obvious stuff that is probably more important than working out – you just got to keep your head right. It's so easy to get spun out. You see people who have no challenges outside of their Hollywood problems come in, and they regularly have meltdowns on set or they turn into a bitch, or they say and do things because they're under pressure or because they think they're something they're not. It's really a trip to be number one on the call sheet and getting a movie like this and it's ... always kind of an inside game and I forget that occasionally.'

With Robert's charismatic performances quickly making it obvious that this was a star-making role, they would have to balance how much visual effects they would use so that Robert's role was not diluted. 'The visual effects are extending the character performance,' said VFX supervisor John Nelson. 'The core is what you get from the actor's face – what you get from looking at Robert – and the extension is the big stuff you can't do any other way.'

Robert told *Starburst* about their plan to make him an anti-communist hero, and described the comic book character's origins. '[Marvel creative lynchpin] Stan Lee did it as a dare, but it was a time there was a very strong anti-establishment, anti-military-industrial, anti-rich-over-thirty energy. For him it was just a huge challenge. They said they got more female fan mail than for all their other heroes combined because there was this sense of him being very vulnerable. This very precarious device that keeps him alive and devours him is clearly a metaphor for something else.'

Lee said his inspiration was Howard Hughes. 'He was an inventor, an adventurer, a multimillionaire, a ladies' man and, finally, a nutcase.'

Created in 1963 and appearing in issue 39 of *Tales of Suspense*, Iron Man was another Marvel hero who was a less-than-perfect crime fighter, as like Superman or, to an extent, Batman were. They had flaws, personal problems and were tonally grey rather than the usual black and white. If the X-Men was rooted in the racial situation that struck America in the 1960s, Iron Man was played against the backdrop of the Cold War – with his many enemies usually revolving around the Russians trying to build a better Iron Man.

However, with the backlash against the American government at an all-time high because of the Vietnam war, the character would become a more socially conscious superhero. It bled through to the

1980s when, thanks to the huge boost in capitalism that revitalised the US, his enemies would normally be rooted in big business. The 1980s also had storylines that would focus on Stark's alcohol problems – a story that would become one of the most iconic comic-book tales of all time.

Terrence Howard was discussed for the title role, but would end up playing Tony Stark's army friend James Rhodes instead. 'For a little while people thought I was going to be Iron Man and it didn't hurt my career at all. I could have done it, but Iron Man's sensibilities would have been a lot different,' said Howard.

'I don't know if he would have been as free thinking and free form as Robert's Iron Man. Robert has a comparative nature – he's been a child of privilege, like Stark's character. He knows what that life is like.'

Clearly overjoyed at landing the role, Robert told *Esquire* magazine, 'Here's how insane life gets – I'm doing a fucking biopic? It's the same pressure as *Chaplin*, except there's no reference.

'Why am I the guy for this job? Because the story is the most duplicitous and conflicted of all the Marvel characters, because he's really just a guy who gets put in an extraordinary set of circumstances – partially due to his own character defects and partially due to his lineage – and you can pick a fucking million Joseph Campbell myths and look 'em up.'

Gwyneth Paltrow, who plays secretary Pepper Potts who has a crush on Tony, added, 'Robert kept me on my toes and kept our on-screen relationship sexually charged. Sometimes I've had to work with people I have had zero chemistry with and it's like pulling teeth. Because sometimes it's just not there and when it is there, it's like flying. It feels like you can do anything and when it's not there, it's a struggle.'

While a very impressive cast was assembled and time was obviously taken on who should play their lead star, the film's script had been neglected, leaving Jeff Bridges (who plays Stark's second-in-command Obadiah Stane) bemused at what he saw. 'They had no script, man,' he told the *Guardian*. 'They had an outline. We would show up for big scenes every day and we wouldn't know what we were going to say. We would have to go into our trailer and work on this scene and call up writers on the phone: "You got any ideas?" Meanwhile the crew is tapping their foot on the stage waiting for us to come on.'

The problems didn't end there. 'You've got the suits from Marvel in the trailer with us saying, "No, you wouldn't say that." You would think with a $200 million movie you'd have the shit together, but it was just the opposite. And the reason for that is because they get ahead of themselves. They have a release date before the script – "Oh, we'll have the script before that time" – and they don't have their shit together.

'Jon [Favreau] dealt with it so well,' Bridges added. 'It freaked me out. I was very anxious. I like to be prepared. I like to know my lines, man, that's my school. Very prepared. That was very irritating and then I just made this adjustment. It happens in movies a lot where something's rubbing against your fur and it's not feeling right, but it's just the way it is. You can spend a lot of energy bitching about that or you can figure out how you're going to do it, how you're going to play this hand you've been dealt. What you can control is how you perceive things and your thinking about it. So I said, "Oh, what we're doing here, we're making a $200 million student film. We're all just fuckin' around! We're playin'. Oh, great!" That took all the pressure off. "Oh, just jam, man – just play." And it turned out great!'

Talking about improv with Bridges, Robert said, 'Jeff came in and he would be like, "Guys, we should improvise on this scene." And we're like, we are shooting in two weeks. We're like still figuring out what the sequences are and we're like, "We got two raptors and he's fighting the F22s and 'what', 'how', 'why'. And Jeff's like, "I got this [Zen Buddhist interpreter] Alan Watts lecture I downloaded on my iPod and we should listen to it." And it's like two hours and ten minutes.

'So anyway, he wound up really, really bringing us to where we felt like we had permission to do what we all wanted to do anyway – which was get to know each other and talk about this stuff. He's like, "I'm not fixing the show up right here and being like that two-dimensional bad guy." But what kind of happens is he's like The Dude meets Doctor Doom. It's awesome. We talk about that Tocamac reactor. Every time we got into a thing about, "What does that mean?" it's hard to say what has value when you're in the clinch. It really was just some of my favourite stuff because I've come up and I'm a little younger than Jeff, but he's always someone I've seen as having this very interesting, balanced career. And he's just a national treasure.'

Robert was also very enthusiastic about the film's director. 'Jon Favreau has been very flexible and very fun because we're very similar. Jon and I are treating Tony and through that half the lines are his and half the ideas are mine.' As an example, Robert cited an instance of how Favreau's attitude towards improvisation allowed him to improve the dialogue in a scene he thought didn't work.

'Well, what happened was that they lit it one way and I came and said, "Uh-oh!" Jon's like, "Downey, what is it now? We got to shoot something!" and I was like, "Why? I hate this scene when it's like, 'Mr. Stark! Mr. Stark!' and they all crowd in… [Favreau] is like, "All right, what are you going to do?" And this all starts from the scene before, where originally Tony says, "Pepper, I'm back and I want to have a press conference."

'I was like, "I'm not going to say that. I'll say some other stuff and mix it in with that, but I'm not going to come out and go, 'Goddamn it, Pepper! It's time for a press conference!'" Because I think, "What does he think he has to say?" I don't think he knows what he's going to say.

'Well, anyway, I'm like, "Look, there's two things I want to change." Because it's the truth, I hear, when people come out of the joint and come back from a long sentence. That's what happened with me after we did this world tour and came back to the Waldorf and they were like, "Mister, is there anything you would like on your cheeseburger?" And I said [in answer to Favreau], "Two things – I want a cheeseburger and I want a press conference." So he got what he wanted and I didn't have to hit it.'

Talking about the ending, he added, 'We had no idea how it was going to go at the end. We just figured that by the time we got there, it didn't make sense for him to go out and tell the cover story with the camera. We tried to do everything else so counter-intuitively at that point, so that day there was a choice and Jon was like, "We should just let the cat out of the bag because that's our way." We took all these things in a very, very simple and well-plotted origin story and then we tried to flip the expectation as often as we could.

'Jon and I have become brothers,' he added. 'We're practically like each other's wives when our wives aren't there. But what always is interesting me about any ideas is who I'm working with and how far we can take this.'

When Robert filmed his cameo as Tony Stark in *The Incredible Hulk* alongside William Hurt, the latter revealed, "We improv'd that. The entire scene had no lines written down. We did improv for that entire scene. We actually both had more of a script because of that and a feeling of more invention because of that. So we could actually go, "OK, who do I think my character is? What would he say next? I haven't a clue – let's have a shot at it.'

On its release, *Iron Man* was a box-office smash – and to say thanks, Marvel Studios chairman David Maisel bought Robert a £100,000 Bentley. *Guardian* journalist Philip French spoke for many critics when he raved that Robert had once again proved he was 'one of the most versatile, attractive and gifted actors in America today'.

Robert said, 'It's great to see a sold-out audience that you know is made up of comic book fans and people who had never read an *Iron Man* comic in their life.'

With the film showing him off to a whole new generation of film fans, he took great pleasure in Googling himself. "Oh, I love all that shit, personally. Sorry. I just love it. Because it's a hoot. Some people overstate their support, like they know you,' the *Daily Express* quoted him as saying. 'Other people are busy doing something else and just want to go on this chat site and say some despicable character assassination, which I honestly think they kind of nailed. I do have that shortcoming. It's really fun.'

Robert, however, was not going to get carried away by the movie's success and played down the effect it might have on his career. 'I think it's like anything. At a certain point, Favreau and I were invited to a dinner at a Chinese restaurant in Beverly Hills and I felt like they opened the books and we were made guys. There was a lot of, like, power players there and studio people ... and we left and I felt "we were just like mafia. They just made us." It was this weird thing too because I don't know if any of us had this experience, but sometimes you go from being in one position to being in another or you have a certain sense of achievement and there's this kind of energy that happens where there literally is an energetic transformation. Then the next day you wake up and it's just another day.'

He added, 'I'm between two phases right now, pre-*Iron Man* and post-*Iron Man* and the transition can be tricky. It used to be: I'd drive onto a studio lot and the guard was like, "*Less Than Zero*, dude. I loved *Chaplin*!" Now it's, "*Iron Man!*" It's not an algorithm any more. It's a fixed number. Things have been zeroed out; it's the beginning of something. But right now, it's still a void and we tend to think of the void as an abyss or a vacuum with nothing there. In fact, it's a new road and what you should do on this new road is close for repairs – close right away, because that old vehicle is not going to work on that new road.

'I mean, if the cosmos is a loving, healing thing that also spins real fast and erupts and does violent stuff, and if there really is some kind of order to the whole thing, then everything that's led up to this moment has to be part of it, or the math doesn't work. But in this transition phase, I really am trying to live as much like a lizard as I can. Hot rock, sun, fly, tongue.

'Right now, my BlackBerry is literally overloading and crashing and the phone is never not ringing. It's crazy. Like a Super Bowl. Like a landslide. Like nothing I've ever experienced.'

With the film's success and his career not only back on track but charging ahead in express fashion, there was only one thing to say. 'Life is great.'

16

ROBERT STEALS EVERYONE'S THUNDER

*'I have never been happier for someone
else's success in my life'*
BEN STILLER

With *Iron Man*'s success launching Robert into the stratosphere, he should have been feeling proud, vindicated and ecstatic. It was rage, however, that was foremost in his mind.

'I have to say that when things turned for me, there was an inclination, an impulse for revenge that was fucking palpable. Palpable. Though it had nothing to do with any particular person, it was really kind of alarming. I hadn't been aware of having a vindictive bone in my body. But once all that water of being hugely self-destructive went under the bridge, to see that what's left is this fucking dark shit, this capacity for random revenge – well, it's just so weird. It's weird, dude. It's weird. Life is weird.'

Robert was on vacation with his wife in Hawaii when a friend told him, 'Hey, Stiller's in town – you might want to give him a call.'

Comedian-writer-director-producer Ben Stiller was looking for an actor to star in his latest project, the action-comedy *Tropic Thunder*. Set in the jungle of Vietnam, it's the story of a group of actors playing soldiers in a war movie, who are forced to rescue one of their number after he is kidnapped by drug-growing locals who mistake them for real soldiers. The part Stiller was looking to fill was that of Kirk Lazarus – an actor (reportedly modelled on Russell Crowe) who has been hailed as one of the greatest of all time. He takes his craft incredibly seriously and for this new war film he gets a controversial cosmetic operation to turn his skin black.

Stiller said, 'You had to believe that his character Kirk Lazarus is the greatest actor of his generation and we had to find somebody for the role who actually is a serious actor that was respected, otherwise it wouldn't have any weight to the character. Who else could be that funny and taken seriously as an actor?'

Robert was close to turning down *Tropic Thunder*, however, because he wasn't keen on shooting two films back to back.

'A lot of people do big movies back to back,' Stiller urged him.

'Yeah, but I'm not a lot of people,' Robert replied. 'I've got to be careful here.'

Once on board, though, Robert went all out. As Stiller recalled, 'We all have our demons and stuff, but I've never seen anybody get lit for the acting moment as much as him. He was in a crazy zone and totally committed to his character.

'Downey improvised so much,' he added. 'He really hit a groove with the character. I think it was very freeing for him to be this Australian guy who obviously had so much talent but focused so much on his roles he could never be himself. So much of what's on the screen came from those improvisation sessions. He was like the biggest bargain genius actor on the planet.'

Robert talked to the *Daily Record* about the attraction of doing *Tropic Thunder*. 'I wanted to work with Ben and Jack Black, but my way into the movie is that I may have my reputation destroyed. The whole idea of actors taking themselves seriously is the funniest thing I've ever seen. When I was thinking about Kirk Lazarus, I was thinking about Colin Farrell, Daniel Day-Lewis and Russell Crowe.

'At the end of the day, it's always about how well you commit to the character. I dove in with both feet. If I didn't feel it was morally sound, or that it would be easily misinterpreted that I'm just C Thomas Howell in [1980s misfire] *Soul Man*, I would've stayed home.'

To help him develop the character, Robert drew on the memory of his dad's time working on *Putney Swope*. 'As soon as I got the role in *Tropic Thunder*, I started thinking about my dad's movie. I remember when he was making it, guys from the Black Panthers came over to our house. They were cool, they just wanted to keep him in check.

'I remembered their voices and the voices of my black friends growing up and I kind of used it for *Tropic Thunder*. I had this husky voice for three months and the film was the most beautiful, kind of cathartic experience for me.'

Talking further about getting into character, Robert said, 'Give me an accent, I've got a character. I don't have to do anything else. Put whatever clothes on me you want. If I'm worrying about the pants or the hair or the dialogue, I must: a) not have an accent; or b) not be in a good movie.'

One of the film's stars, Brandon T Jackson, recalled, 'We'd be watching a monitor and he just kept going on about, "I'm going to get me some barbecued ribs and chicken," and I'm like, "No, man, you can't do that. You gotta stop that, for real." But he just kept on and then when we were doing the scene where I get pissed off at him, all that stuff just came out there and magic happened. I don't know, but I think in his genius he was just trying to egg me on.'

It was an incredibly brave role for Robert to play, when you consider how easily it could have gone wrong. His agents must have wanted to tear their hair out. He had just starred in one of the biggest movie hits of the year and here he was taking a risk when he would have been asked to play it safe. But that wasn't Robert's way.

'I thought it was a ridiculous and potentially incendiary idea,' he said. 'If it goes well, maybe you open up the *LA Times* and it says that Robert Downey Jr is flat-out hilarious, like it did this morning. Or you're vilified for having made a decision to do something that people thought was offensive.'

'If Downey thinks something is going to be offensive, it's going to tempt him to do it,' said James Toback.

The controversy Robert had feared failed to materialise. When early pictures of Robert in character were published (it took two hours to put on the make-up), it seemed to generate a lot of interest in the film, which went on to enjoy huge success and Robert was nominated for an Oscar and a BAFTA for his performance.

Robert insisted, 'I don't want to say that we had much moral integrity, but Ben and I had some earnest discussions about what's funny isn't what's offensive and what's self-deprecating. People are used to that and that doesn't necessarily translate to, "Oh, now we actually like you – the person, the actor – because you're sending yourself up."

'It's kind of a little passé. A lot of the humour in this is really just an Americanised twenty-first-century version of the highbrow side of *Monty Python*. It's nothing new. That's why I think that England, the UK and Europe is a very apt market for it – it's nothing shocking.'

Robert was like a kid in a sweet shop. He remembers looking at the posters for *Tropic Thunder* emblazoned everywhere – with him sharing centre stage with major stars like Jack Black and Ben Stiller. Before, he had been one of the supporting actors who had threatened to be more an appetising starter than an A-list main course. But now he was front row and centre. He would stare at the posters, muttering, 'Wow, it's just so nice to be in the game. It's just so nice to be in the game.'

When Stiller cast Robert, he had no idea that it would be Robert who would be the biggest draw, but the box-office success of *Iron Man* changed all that.

'I told Robert I have never been happier for someone else's success in my life,' Stiller said. 'After working with him, I'd do anything for him. He's in a place in his life where he's so committed to working hard, who is grateful for what he has. We were out in the jungle where it was humid and raining, he had on this wig and this make-up and he was the first guy to show up on the set and always ready to go again when another actor flubbed a line. For a director, you can't imagine how important that intangible generosity is, to have an actor that's brilliant who doesn't hold that over everybody.'

It is obvious that Stiller and Robert had chemistry, and they had the audience in stitches when they introduced clips from the movie at the major movie-industry convention ShoWest, as this transcript shows.

Stiller: 'You know what my son said to me? He said, "Daddy, you're my superhero."'

Robert: 'You know what he said to me? "Robert, you're a real superhero – not like my daddy, who's a fake superhero."'

Stiller: 'Obviously you didn't see a little movie I did called *Mystery Men*.'

Robert: 'Uh? *Mystery Men*? Is that a real movie? I must have missed that one...'

Stiller: 'You must have been in jail when it came out. Maybe they didn't show that in Gen Pop.'

Robert: 'You know what my son said to me? He said he's having recurring nightmares.'

Stiller: 'Oh really? Why?'

Robert : 'He dreamed we had to go and watch *The Heartbreak Kid* again.'

Stiller: 'You know, that's not funny.'

Proof of the influence Susan had on Robert came when he found out that he had a whole day of press for *Tropic Thunder* coming up. After he'd complained, she said, 'Let me tell you, you can complain all you want, but it's Ben and you're going to do it. So if it feels good to build up a lot of resentment and rage, fine. But with all due respect, it's not that big a deal. You're not performing surgery during each of those events. You're standing there fucking looking hot.'

There was talk of a possible sequel but Robert was dismissive of the idea. 'I have a feeling that we'd still make some money but it probably wouldn't be as good,' he said. '[But] I would like to work with Ben again.'

17

ROBERT GETS DRAMATIC

'I've been that train wreck and I've been
that person next to that train wreck'
ROBERT DOWNEY JR

Robert was working on *Tropic Thunder* when director Joe Wright arrived in Hawaii to try to convince him to star in the drama *The Soloist*. Based on a real life story, it's about the unlikely friendship between a journalist and a musically gifted homeless man in one of LA's most dangerous ghettos.

It was 2005 when Steve Lopez discovered 58-year-old Nathaniel Ayers playing music with only two strings on his violin. 'I heard such beautiful music,' Lopez remembered. 'I thought, "OK, where did this all begin? How does this guy end up on this street corner?"'

Ayers told him that he had been to the prestigious Juilliard music academy in New York, and Lopez was stunned to discover that his story was true. Ayers had attended the famous school in 1970. However, in his third year he had suffered a breakdown, with doctors diagnosing him with schizophrenia. He had ended up in LA after wrongly believing that his father was living there after his mother's death.

Touched by his story, Lopez began featuring Ayers in his columns, and it wasn't long before his readers began expressing their interest in him. 'Readers got very involved in the story and began rooting for him,' said Lopez. 'In my thirty-five years as a journalist no one has had a deeper impact on me. He has a passion few of us can ever hope to find. He has introduced me to the music of his gods.'

The journalist then went on to write the book *The Soloist: A Lost Dream, an Unlikely Friendship and the Redemptive Power of Music*, about his relationship with Ayers and his attempts to get him off Skid Row.

'Joe and I had spoken before and I knew that I would be playing a journalist again,' Robert said. 'I wasn't sure, at first, that I wanted to go there. [But] Joe was really passionate about the way they were going to tell this extraordinary story and I was soon convinced. Moreover, I was in the middle of doing this huge, very different kind of movie – and you couldn't be any broader or bigger than *Tropic Thunder* – so the idea of really switching gears and doing something where Joe said he wanted me there every day was appealing.'

Now, everyone wanted a piece of Robert. He even got to meet one of his heroes – Steven Spielberg. 'I couldn't believe it. He's over by the monitors and I'm like, "Jesus Christ – there he is." He talks to me about a couple of things and then he leaves the set, and I'm like, "Goddarn it! I've only been waiting twenty-five years to have one of those moments."'

Talking about *The Soloist* possibly being a last hurrah for journalism, much like the recent *State of Play*, Robert said, 'Particularly when we were doing this last year, the newspapers were seeming like they might be becoming outmoded and all these lay-offs and stuff.

'In some ways the film feels like a love story,' he added. 'A platonic love story, of course. But it's also about faith – about believing in that connection between people and to me that means believing in ourselves. It's funny to say this about what I guess is a big Hollywood movie, but actually it feels like something more personal, something quite pure.

'Because their relationship transcended the book and even the movie, they're still hanging out now. It's not like once the movie rights were bought he said, "Hey, my job is done," or whatever in that typical LA fashion. I think that's what attracted us too. We knew that these were good people who became friends in the most unlikely circumstances.'

Robert was told by Wright to meet as many people as possible from Skid Row and from the Lamp

Community, an LA charity that helps people who have mental illnesses and are homeless.

'Joe wanted to pepper the cast with actual members of the Lamp Community and wanted it to be a film not about mental illness but about faith,' Robert told the *Western Mail*. 'He kept telling me, "The movie is not about you. The movie has nothing to do with you. The movie is about Jamie and these people," and I was like, "Well, then what the hell do you want me there for?" Joe would say, "Robert, just observe." I thought, "Oh God, this guy is so artsy."

'And it turned into this incredibly, wonderfully humbling three months on Skid Row, which is exactly what I needed. Those people are us, so it was like working with us in very trying circumstances. The only way I can describe it was that it was like having dinner with a family during the siege on Stalingrad. The human nature comes forth and people strive and crave to be connected to each other and be like each other, which we are.

'I've been that train wreck and I've been that person next to that train wreck. I can't think of anyone who doesn't relate to the metaphor of derailment and just how awful and tragic that is.'

After meeting the real-life journalist, Robert said, 'Steve is very charming and a great story-teller but, when we met, he insisted that I didn't try to impersonate him in any way, so we ended up going in a different direction. Joe and I talked about trying to create a sense of a man in crisis and that crisis is matched, mirrored and somewhat healed by this incredible relationship with Nathaniel Ayers.'

He added, 'I never listen to anything anyone says about what I should or shouldn't do. I know he said it would be a mistake to impersonate him and there wasn't time and it wasn't my job. I felt like my job was to observe and report and Joe Wright said I needed to witness this movie, which was very odd, because I had so been the centre of attention in a very overt way in a couple things I'd done before. So to me, it was about having the humility to do what we are supposed to do as actors all the time, which is just be there and imagine that that's enough.'

At a certain point when Robert and Lopez weren't quite sure what the boundaries were, Robert asked if he could make a replica of Lopez's nose. 'We cast his nose. I said, "Let me see what Steve's nose looks like on me. God, I kind of like that." And Joe said, "Robert…" because I'd gotten used to all of this armature. I had had a suit on, or was African-American and my mask was really easy. So I was asked not to do that.'

Looking back on the movie, Robert stated, 'I think *The Soloist* is interesting in that it talks about massive conflicts with the self in a normal state of being and with the world in a chaotic state of being. It's such a simple story. As Joe Wright rightly says, I am observing – and I am in denial of my conflict.'

He added, 'That sense of having true empathy and compassion is realising not just "There but for the grace of God go I" but also, even with our contradictions and traumas and shortcomings and things that are remiss and regrets, that we all have the fortune to operate in a fundamentally sane realm. The idea of being forever uncontained is such a wrenching prospect and yet there are still ways we can connect with each other and embrace.

'Mel Gibson has a fantastic phrase: "You gotta hug the cactus." I think that's what it is. Faith that there's value in hugging the cactus. It's a necessity. It's unavoidable.'

And what did real Nathaniel Ayers make of all this? Talking about the premiere, he said, 'I listened to the film but I did not watch it. I was wearing a blindfold. I don't really watch films – I prefer to concentrate on my music. I only went to the premiere because people had gone to so much trouble over me. It was incredible what they put on. People were shouting, "Look over here!" and "Over here, Nathaniel!" I have never been so honoured in all my life.

'But I got to shake hands with Mr Jamie Foxx. I took the blindfold off right before I met him. And I shook hands with Mr Robert Downey Jr too.'

Had he been rewarded for what was, after all, the story of his life?

'I didn't want anything from them,' Ayers said. 'They bought me this cello and a trumpet, a nice new guitar. But other than that, the financial side didn't really come into it. After all, what is money to me other than the dollar I need to buy a hotdog on Main Street? I didn't want to have any handouts.

'It's amazing what has happened to me. I am so thankful, especially to Mr Steve Lopez. Everything that has happened, it's like a dream come true.'

The Soloist is the sort of project that actors make after achieving commercial or award-winning success. It's an inspiring drama, handsomely made and impeccably performed. However, this type of film rarely makes an impression at the box office. For Robert to keep his appeal, he needed a project that would excite cinemagoers. His next film would have mainstream appeal but – Robert not being one to rest on his laurels – it would also be a typically bold and somewhat risky choice.

18

ELEMENTARY MY DEAR ROBERT

Just as Robert had grown up with Chaplin and Iron Man, so Sherlock Holmes was an important part of director Guy Ritchie's childhood.

'I've felt an investment in the character of Sherlock Holmes since I was six years old,' Ritchie said, 'because I was sent to boarding school at six, until I was ten. It was the longest period I've been at any school. There were little speakers inside the dormitories and if the kids were good, at night the only stories they'd play were Sherlock Holmes – I think eight-track tapes or whatever. I mean, it's two geezers acting in a room with a bit of "clickity-clack", but I was keenly aware of the significance of the intellect and the drama within their narrative.

'And if the kids fucked about too much, what

they'd do is flick off the narrative and then whoever was responsible for it being flicked off would have something of the blanket party descend upon them.'

Interestingly, the latest adaptation of Sherlock Holmes wasn't inspired by Sir Arthur Conan Doyle's famous books but by a comic book. It all started when movie producer Lionel Wigram became obsessed with making a modern retelling of the detective that would not present him as 'a fuddy duddy *Masterpiece Theatre* guy'. However, he knew that his vision might not be clear enough to pitch to Hollywood. What he needed was striking images to support his story outline. On the recommendation of an executive at DC Comics, he turned to the British artist John Watkiss and paid him $5,000 to draw up several scenes.

'What he drew was what I imagined, but better,' Wigram said. 'And if you compare Guy Ritchie's screen version to the images, there's a direct connection. Watkiss deserves a lot of credit and recognition for this.'

Wigram published the images and several story points into a small number of comic books to pitch to the studio, with Warner Bros eventually becoming the studio to take on the film.

Joel Silver was the producer on the movie and once again he would find himself working with Robert. The actor jokingly enquired to the producer, 'Dude, where's our franchise?' and was stunned when Silver came back to him almost straight away with the idea of showing off Holmes to a whole new generation.

'And then Joel and I got excited, and me and the Mrs [Susan, who was a producer on the movie], we like separateness within unity. We love working together and that has always been a fruitful thing. So, we knew it had to be done in period. We knew that we had to really roll up our sleeves and do it justice because what would be lamer than doing a version of Sherlock Holmes, given that opportunity to either sail or dump the franchise for any future takers, by making a version of it that isn't quite smart enough?

'So we really wanted to make it without being too clever for its own good. We wanted to really root it in what we love about these characters and we wanted it to also be as exciting as what's required nowadays for a big movie.'

Robert had adored Ritchie's *RocknRolla* and thought he was a perfect fit for the new interpretation of Holmes. However, the way Robert tells it, Guy took some convincing that he was the right guy for it. 'Here's kind of what happened. I called Guy because I'd seen *RocknRolla* and clearly I was between jobs. I might be wrong but at the time I think he said, "You might be a little old for it!" But like I said, I had a hell of a summer and had a very stern conversation with him...

'But as it turns out, I think we're really well suited to work together. Looking into the books, the more I looked, the more fantastic it is … the fact that he is a student of some kind of nebulous martial arts. He's just such a weirdo. As a matter of fact, Mrs Downey said that when you read the description of the guy … as quirky and nuts as it is, it could be a description of me on some days. But I'm gonna do it better than it's ever been done before.'

Announcing the film to the world, Robert told a packed press conference, 'A hundred and twenty-two years ago, Sir Arthur Conan Doyle gave birth to a character. He was probably the first superhero. He was an intellectual superhero. And he was also the first Western martial artist, I'm told, and probably one of the most recognisable images, icons, names on Earth. So much so that a lot of people actually think, or thought for the most part, that Sherlock Holmes was a real guy.

'There's been a myriad TV shows and film and series done on Sherlock Holmes, but I just scratch my head and go, "I can't believe this hasn't been brought back into mainstream nowadays." I thought, "Why hadn't they figured it out 'til just yet?" Casting. And Guy Ritchie at the helm, because what we have in Guy Ritchie is a badass gentleman, Englishman, who understands how to reinvigorate something like this. We have the ever-delectable and seriously gifted Rachel McAdams playing Irene Adler, the only woman that ever worked Sherlock like a rib. And, of course, Jude Law as Watson.

Talking about working with Susan, he said, 'I know

my place! We love working together. Making movies is so energy- and time-consuming that it takes you away from your real life for big chunks of time. So I get to escape with her, as opposed to from her.'

Ritchie would say that the couple were 'the greatest illustration of a symbiotic marriage that I've ever seen. It's a real yin and yang and it's made him a joy to work with. Robert would be a pain in the ass if he didn't have Susan to police him.'

Jude Law, who played Holmes' sidekick Dr Watson, said, 'When I was asked to get involved, Robert was already set as Sherlock and Guy was directing. I knew from then that it was going to be a different take than the older films of Sherlock Holmes and it fascinated me. Obviously they were coming to me not to put on two stone and fool around and not to put my foot in wastepaper baskets – they were coming to ask me to play Watson with a bit more edge. What was intriguing – because I hadn't read the books as a boy – was to go back to the books and realise how much of this new rediscovery, if you like, was also in the source material.

'So, it was kind of a happy juggle between going back to Conan Doyle and relishing all the inaccuracy that perhaps in times past had been overlooked, and also looking to the future and adding a new energy to an audience that we hope will rediscover a new Sherlock Holmes or discover Sherlock Holmes for the first time.'

Speaking about Law, Robert said, 'I always think that I'm the most all-around gifted person on any project. I have to do that – otherwise I'll start to crumble. By the time I saw Jude in *Hamlet*, I remember thinking, "He may have more tools in his box than [I do]."'

Robert and Law would bond at Guy Ritchie's co-owned pub, the Punch Bowl, in posh Mayfair. They would spend hours there on a handful of occasions, getting to know each other.

Robert said, 'I think the more we all looked into the original lexicon of the four novels and the dozens and dozens of short stories, the more we realised that, in a way, Sherlock had been misrepresented in a lot of the previous, much-loved televised and film entertainment versions. I think some of it was a constraint of just the times, because he was very kind of liberal and trippy and all that stuff.

'But every time we were in doubt, Susan, Rachel, Lionel and Joel and I – and Jude was very central in this too – we would go back to what Doyle said these people said, and how did these people describe each other? Because there are trillions of pages of data about Holmes, Watson, Adler, the adventures they go on and where they lived, what their likes and dislikes are. So we really went pretty much right back to the source. That was how we reinvigorated it – by deciding to change less than had been changed previously.'

It was also a chance for Robert to work in Britain again – a country he has always looked on with fond memories after working there on films like *Chaplin* and *Restoration*. However, he concedes that there were some cultural difficulties.

Talking to *Hollywood Reporter*, he said, 'We'd call a story meeting and Susan and I would just launch into the myriad subjects we need to attack to make the script better, and we'd look up at Guy and his British buddies or department heads. They'd kind of look at us as though they didn't want to make us feel bad but were mildly disgusted with how uncivilised we were about just launching right into work.

'So I was like, "Susan, why don't we get a cheese plate and a little of that low- to mid-grade caviar … maybe somebody wants a blini. It's tea time, isn't it? Well, let's see if they want some tea." And no sooner did we start opening our sessions with an offer of a beverage or some food – as soon as we civilised ourselves – the floodgates of goodwill opened.'

Asked about Holmes' supposed trademark – the deerstalker hat – Robert said, 'There is one occasion in all of the reference material where he wore one. One time. For one scene. In one of the books [*The Adventure of Silver Blaze*]. And the big, curved pipe was not from [Holmes actor Basil] Rathbone or any of these guys. When William Gillette played him in theatre, he wanted a pipe that didn't obscure his face. Otherwise, Holmes smoked a straight black clay pipe.'

Near the start of the film, audiences would see a whole new side to Holmes – that of a bare-knuckle fighter. When these pictures surfaced before the film's release, fans of the character worried that Ritchie's take was too much like the director's previous gang-style films.

Robert remembered, 'There was a choreographed version of it that I went in and got all pissy about. Then Guy came in and we worked on it. So, I think you were probably seeing version six by the time we shot it. Guy is a jujitsu fellow. We managed to get along somehow. It was so fun. By the time we were done shooting that and doing that scene I felt we really had a handle on the movie – not because we'd finally top-lit me and I'd shown my rippling abs and all that, but this was Guy's idea of Holmes' vision and it was a really bold thing.

'It could have gone very poorly, in which case the rest of the movie is trying to recover from the bad Guy Ritchie idea that we went out and shot. It was literally perfect and I think it set the tone. It was just his take on the film so it was about me trusting him and us getting each other's approval so to speak.'

The action scenes would see Robert throw himself into the picture, with one incident seeing him needing hospital treatment. 'We developed a lot of [the choreography] early on, and some of it was very dialled in. But often as not we'd get there and say, "This doesn't feel quite right." We'd pull out as many toys as we had that were clad in rubber and start swinging. I only really got rocked once and I needed less than ten stitches. We actually still finished the day and then I went to the hospital.'

The injury was just on the inside of Robert's lip. 'It was no big deal. But I was very happy when Guy said it was more serious than he thought. That really made my day because he would routinely show up on set with black eyes from his [marital arts] training.'

Rachel McAdams, who played Irene Adler (Holmes's love interest), said, 'I wasn't that shocked [to hear that Robert got stitches] because he gives so much, like he goes a hundred and ten per cent. When I heard he got punched in the face I thought he probably asked for it: "That doesn't look real, punch me again."'

Elaborating on her own character, McAdams added, 'Well, Irene is really fun because she's totally a kind of woman for the late 1800s. She's very independent. She's very active. She kind of lives in the underworld. There's only one story where Irene is introduced, "Scandal in Bohemia", and it's a really fun story between her and Sherlock. She happens to beat Sherlock at his own game and it's the first time a woman has ever done that.

'So we developed this kind of strange love affair,' McAdams said with a laugh, 'a very unique love affair. We just kind of played on that, but we're very competitive with one another and we're trying to outsmart each other all the time, yet trying to have this odd, normal relationship, which is nearly impossible. It's fun.'

Making compelling action scenes were important to Robert. 'I've seen a bunch of movies where you think, "Here comes the big action sequence and there's the explosion and..." In this film, we just keep talking about, "How do we keep these characters alive during these big sequences?" We're really working our butts off to get the script, the action, the overall look of the film to super, super high quality – to make a really solid piece of entertainment, because I think audiences are too savvy and they'll get pissed off if we talk up this great movie and then we don't really deliver.'

Ritchie wasn't a product of the Hollywood system and his set reflected that. Robert described it as verging on chaos and found 'something so relaxed about that'. Robert is something of a kinetic, hyperactive person who is prone to mood swings, and he always works better in an environment suited to his needs. It's not so much about catering for his talents as acting like a light switch in his creative brain.

It was a tough and frantic shoot, with Robert saying they worked their 'asses off' on the movie. 'We worked weekends. We worked after work. We worked in the thing. We took it really, really, really seriously. And I think that's why we're so proud.

'It was really up to us how far we wanted to explore

and how exhaustingly we wanted to do rewrites and all that other stuff. And McAdams and I really would slave away over a hot, empty piece of text in the trailer when they were essentially set-up on stage and we were just wondering what else we could do. And then sometimes we'd lock into stuff and it would really work.

'But I guess the challenging thing was that it was controlled chaos. It was very civilised. It was a largely British production and I was a little embarrassed coming back to the States because we're just like, "Work! Die! Die! Die working!" And they're like, "Let's just have a spot of tea and then we'll move on." So there was this rhythm that was created where the opportunity was on us. Lionel [Wigram], Susan and I spent so many hours really just thinking, "Let's look in the Holmes encyclopaedia. Let's look in this list of quotations." And we always found stuff there, but it was such a deep treasure trove that the big challenge was recognising how tough it was to get it right and doing it anyway.'

As he added succinctly to the *Japan Times*, 'It was a long shoot. No major dramas. People got along. We went in there and worked. And then we worked some more.'

Talking about working with Guy Ritchie, Susan Downey said, 'Guy is a character. Joel and I had worked with him on *RocknRolla* but obviously this is a much bigger movie – the scope of the movie, the time we had to shoot it, the money we had to make it and all that. And what's really great about Guy is he has a sense of what the feel, the vibe, the tone is going to be, which is what you'll see reflected in his movies. He was also very conscious that he was being given an opportunity to show kind of a different side of himself as a director. So I think you're going to recognise his sense of style, but it's going to be brought to a whole new level.

'What we observed of Guy working with the actors is that he gives them a lot of leeway. There are parameters, but he lets them do their thing. He'll watch and then he'll come in, and if he likes it he'll let them just go with it. And if he doesn't, everybody clears out and he steps in. He puts his writer's hat on, sits with them and hammers it out until we get the scene right.

'And he's one of the most efficient directors we've ever worked with. He's very time-conscious, sometimes to the point where you're like, "Dude, just take the time you need. We'll make it work." But sometimes he'll just be like, "Come on, come on – we have the crew ready, we've got to go. Let's just get it right." But he's really good about coming in and tweaking and shaping, but he lets everybody else do their jobs. He's not one of those directors who's going to micro-manage.'

Joel Silver was, as ever, enthusiastic about the work of the actor he'd championed through the hard times.

'Downey really is genius in this role,' he said. 'He's genius in every role, but he really made it come to life.'

However, Robert's insistence on hinting at Sherlock's homosexuality caused a bit of a stir in the US. In January 2009, he pondered on a chat show whether or not the character was a 'very butch homosexual'. Afterwards, the woman who holds the US rights to Sherlock Holmes, Andrea Plunket, said, 'I hope this is just an example of Mr Downey's black sense of humour. It would be drastic, but I would withdraw permission for more films to be made if they feel that is a theme they wish to bring out in the future. I am not hostile to homosexuals, but I am to anyone who is not true to the spirit of the books.'

Robert was unrepentant, telling Welt Online, 'I didn't beat about the bush. First of all, I know a lot of heterosexual men who are more effeminate than my gay friends. Some of those are the toughest guys I've known. But I don't want to evade. I did my homework – I did a lot of research about Holmes. You inevitably come across a homosexual subtext. I don't know if Conan Doyle intended it. If so, he was ahead of the times.'

While Robert was keen to allude to the detective's sexuality, the film-makers were less happy to explore Holmes' drug habit in the film. 'I don't know if you want the kids to buy the action figures of Holmes and

Watson lying on their sides sharing a hookah tube,' Robert joked to *Shortlist*.

Sherlock Holmes' success proved Robert's rising marketability as a movie star and his performance was rewarded with a Golden Globe. However, when an actor famed for more alternative fare enters the mainstream, inevitably there are accusations of selling out.

'If the material is still good and you still like to work with the people – why not?' was Robert's response. '*Sherlock Holmes* was a life-changing experience. That's due to the extensive research we did and because I could actually realise such a big project. I would still play characters like Sherlock in the future. Although, I will probably have another child and an alcohol-free vineyard by then.'

19

ROBERT STILL GOING STRONG

*'I was hesitant about a sequel but we've
got something pretty special going'*
ROBERT DOWNEY JR

In October 2008, it was announced that there would
be an *Iron Man 2*. Producer Kevin Feige said, 'It has
already become apparent as we prep the movie for
production that the dynamic between Robert and
[new recruit] Don [Cheadle] will take *Iron Man 2* to
new heights.'

Cheadle had replaced Howard in the movie after a
reported salary dispute. Howard told Parade.com,
'They produced a great bounty with the first one, but
they put it all in the storehouse and you were not
allowed in. They did the same thing with Gwyneth
Paltrow, from what I've been told. They did it with
everyone but Robert Downey.

'I've seen the script,' he added. 'I know what's going to happen, but I'm not revealing anything. I believe in karma. When someone does something wrong, you don't have to get them back. Everything right will return the favour for you. I'm definitely looking forward to seeing the movie. I want to see Don Cheadle become me. No, I want him to do better than me. That's what I really want to see. Don Cheadle was the reason I got *Crash*, so I have a lot of love for him.' Howard dispelled any notion that he was bitter about his exit, saying after the movie was released, 'I haven't had a chance yet but I will see *Iron Man 2*. Despite the customary idea or thought that there's some controversy, it was a wonderful split and I know that they've done well. Robert Downey Jr was born to play that part and it was wonderful that that part has given him the stature that he was supposed to hold before.'

Favreau heaped praise on Robert's contribution to *Iron Man 2*. 'Robert is a real partner in the process. He's been very involved in the screenplay. When he went away to do *Sherlock Holmes* he was still part of our creative process. Even in the first film, where he was originally a hired gun playing the role, he really stepped up to rewrite scenes. He's a great writer, too. So we really are sharing the responsibilities.'

Robert added, 'We are grinding our minds and hearts in the ground on this movie. Could we have just skated through a sequel and would it probably have made the same box-office numbers? Yes, sure.

'I have fortified my belief that if I have a creative instinct about something, usually it's not because I've had too much coffee or because I'm bored – it's because I sense there's something there. And it's always mind blowing when you follow a hunch and realise it's exactly what the movie wanted.'

The first film had been a huge success, but it was also an unexpected one. And Favreau knew that the parameters had changed. 'The first film had the charm of the original story and a new cast being introduced. People expected nothing of us and we over-delivered. Now the question is, can we deliver what people expect and then break those expectations as well? If you don't do either one, they're either bored or disappointed.'

Talking more about the creative opportunities to do something different in *Iron Man 2*, Favreau said, 'The fact that our hero has no secret identity – that opens up a lot of things for us creatively. The superhero genre has been picked over pretty thoroughly with all the different titles, sequels, reboots. It's tough to keep it fresh and not do something that is derivative of something someone else has done. By taking a left turn at the end of the first film and making him a public figure, it opened it up to a whole lot of new possibilities. It goes beyond your standard secret-identity/caped-crusader model.

'It allowed us to draw upon our experiences and certainly Robert's experiences. Robert had strong points of view on these things. He was propelled quite publicly to a much more successful station and we were able to draw upon that. We were able to comment on the phenomenon of celebrity as we know it today.

'Usually the hero is forced to live an even more bifurcated existence between the esteemed persona of the superhero version of himself and the humble or disguised existences of his secret-identity self. Those twin stories deviate more and more as the hero becomes more established. The hero starts to leave behind the secret identity. All of these franchises struggle to find their different angle on all of that as they move forward, but the thing is it's all fairly limited and limiting. There are only so many stories there. We're flying in a different direction.'

Mickey Rourke said, 'I normally don't care for that type of film but I saw the first one and they very much took a chance by having somebody like Robert Downey Jr – who's not your conventional action hero – play the role. I thought that was pretty bold and it paid off. Robert brought a quirky and unpredictable sense of humour to it. He didn't make it stereotypical like *Spider-Man*, like *Batman* and all that shit.'

Robert returned the compliment. 'How badass was Mickey with those whips? But, really, at the end of the day, it's just two schmucks in trailers and once in a while I'd be like, "Hey, mind if I used your treadmill?" And Mickey goes, "Yeah, you should try

my weight vest. Helps you break the sweat quicker."
And I'd be, "OK. See you on set, bad guy," and he'd
say, "OK, punk."

'I'm not fully a Method guy but I like playing
around with that energy sometimes. And Mickey
wanted to do his part in Russian: he had a dialect
coach who taught him and translated, so that was a
very unique take. From the very start, he said, "I don't
want it to be Dolph Lundgren from *Rocky*. I want to
bring humanity and dimensions into it." And I think
he did that.

'He would have someone holding pictures of
recently deceased pets off-camera to make him feel
sad or whatever for a scene. It was all serious stuff.
I've never seen anything like it. But we had a great
time and we were very lucky to get him.'

As Robert had had difficulties because of his
baggage on the first movie, Rourke experienced the
same problem on the follow-up: 'I didn't really know
him but both Robert and Favreau went to bat for me
and, let's put it this way, made it so I was able to do
the movie for what I was asking for. There were some
difficulties and they laid their asses on the line for me.
So when I got on the set I was more than obligated to
bring my A game.'

Rourke was to play a Russian scientist who'd been
incarcerated for many years, and he was determined
to take his research seriously. 'I wanted to go over and
see the facilities in Russia and Russian criminal

society. The inmates were fine and one guy came to my hotel after getting out after twelve years. He showed me these tattoos. They tattoo cats on their fingers or necks and the smaller the kitty cat the more powerful the prisoner. Favreau didn't know I was there but, after, he went to bat for me. I wanted to bring as much back story as I could to the table.'

'And I thought I was eccentric,' said Robert.

Rourke would apply the same intensity while training for the film, donning the aforementioned weight vest on his treadmill. 'The first time I put it on, I had it on for forty minutes and I was to take it off. The whole vest weighed about forty pounds and I would walk twenty-five steps and be exhausted. So what I did with my trainer was put on a forty-pound weight and put the treadmill on uphill and we just worked out for two months.

'It's funny – I'd be on my treadmill and I would see him [Robert] sitting with his vitamins and I thought, "Who would have ever thought the two of us would have not only shown up on time but [been] doing what we were doing?" I'm really happy for his success. He fell off really far and he came back. Just the fact he fell off the ship and was fortunate enough to have the intelligence – he's really bright and the biggest thing is how smart he is.

'The reason why *Iron Man* is so successful is because Favreau took a chance with somebody that has his ability, his sense of humour and his talent, instead of using some young flavour of the month, who just looked good. Robert made the most out of it.'

Sam Rockwell, who plays Iron Man's rival Justin Hammer, was another new addition, with Favreau revealing that he had been in line to play Tony Stark in the first movie. 'He represented a dark-horse idea for Tony Stark early on in the process. A very different take. Of course, when I met with Robert there was nobody else on my mind. There were some things Sam would bring to the role that would have been great. Sam is very charismatic and when I was looking at the character there was a list and he had a spot on it, which might have surprised some people. Robert surprised some people too, though, and now he is Tony Stark. Sam would have come up with interesting and different things.'

The director also revealed that he had chosen Rockwell specifically to pair up with Rourke. 'I went out and purposely hired Sam Rockwell, who is a bit of an unflappable actor, too. He's very poised and he also puts in a good performance, no matter what's going on around him. I had worked with him before and I know that he could hold his own and let Mickey be a strong, brooding type who spoke mostly Russian. I knew Sam could handle the exposition we needed and that's why we added the character of Hammer, who is quite different here than he is in the comics.'

Scarlett Johansson would also star in the movie, as

Natalie, Stark's new personal assistant. Said Robert, 'We were thrilled to get Scarlett and we said to her, "You're not going to be some kind of Marvel spin-off story thing because we want a hot chick kicking ass in this movie," and I think we managed that. A love triangle is a device and a love triangle is convenient and a love triangle – even done badly – is better than not having one at all.'

Paltrow would say of Robert, 'When Scarlett Johansson and I were both on set he was really buzzing. He loves being centre of attention and having his girls around him.'

Robert was rather less fond of the Iron Man suit he had to wear. 'The suit was a little easier this time round, although not enough for my taste,' he said. 'I was physically in the suit twice as much this time as last time. Despite being put under the impression that, with the advances of CGI, it would be three or four days max in the suit, it turned out to be much, much more. Also, I just got older and I came off *Sherlock Holmes*, where I was alarmingly thin, and then proceeded to start pumping up again.

'With this we all wanted to go the extra mile. It is not a nine-to-five job – it's excruciatingly demanding. It is physically demanding too. My character is a master of hand-to-hand combat and there's one particular stunt sequence that we worked on for many months. But our stunt coordinator has been amazing in making me feel I've been doing this my whole life.'

The set was, by all accounts, a charged one – with several reports circulating about on-set disputes. Talking about working with Robert, Rourke replied cryptically, 'He was different every day.'

'If it comes to aggressive outbursts regarding creative particulars, I'm a monster,' Robert conceded. 'I don't mean, like, I act badly or make people feel shitty or anything. But I get really wedged up. It's all I've got in the day, until I get back to my actual life at home.' Tellingly, he then quipped, 'It's all I've got.'

Robert would describe himself and Rourke as 'eccentric', adding in conciliatory fashion, 'The great thing was, before we even got him to agree to do *Iron Man 2* with us, when I would see him around – in Beverly Hills at some Italian joint, or whatever – he always went out of his way to just be cool and have camaraderie with me.'

Like the first movie, *Iron Man 2* was a huge hit at the box office. It might not have impressed the critics as much as the first one – many accused it of being bloated, with too many characters and storylines muddling the picture – but it certainly didn't deter the cinemagoers.

20

ROBERT'S FUTURE

'I've lived more mistakes than I could possibly repeat'
ROBERT DOWNEY JR

What's next for Robert? The comedy *Due Date* – completed and scheduled for release in the US in November 2010 – will see him play a man who must hitchhike across America in a desperate bid to see his child born. There is also the expected appearance of Iron Man in the eagerly awaited *The Avengers*, which will see Iron Man, Nick Fury (Samuel L Jackson), Captain America (Chris Evans) and other Marvel Comics superheroes team up for a series of larger-than-life action adventures – quite a demanding feat to pull off.

'If we don't get it right it's really, really going to suck,' Robert said. 'It has to be the crowning blow of Marvel's best and brightest, because it's the hardest thing to get right. It's tough to spin all the plates for one of these characters.

'I think its important that I do what I'm supposed to do, which is keep my side of the street clean. The danger you run with colliding all these worlds is [because producer-director] Jon [Favreau] was very certain that *Iron Man* should be set in a very realistic world. Nothing that happened in *Iron Man* is really outside the realm of possibility. Once you start talking about Valhalla and super-sized super-soldiers and jolly green giants, it warrants much further discussion.

'There are a lot more invisible eyes on us now. People are going to be more critical. That's their prerogative. In a way, there's no way to win, except to win. Big.'

When making *Iron Man 2*, Favreau said to *Total Film*, 'If I don't do a good job with this one, it jeopardises all future films in the collective Marvel universe. *Iron Man* was the first film to establish the tone of the world. Since Marvel have committed to make the universe, *Iron Man 2* does have a ripple effect into the other movies.

'When I decided to have Nick Fury after the credits in Iron Man, that Easter-egg scene turned into a nine-picture deal for Samuel L Jackson. So these little impulsive decisions that are based on a creative whim have ramifications that affect the entire set of franchises.'

And what about a third *Iron Man* movie? Well, according to Favreau, 'There's an *Iron Man 3*. Here's how I know. When they make the option deals, they include *Iron Man 3*. So I know they're planning on making another one. Whether that would be before or after *The Avengers*, I don't know. They've announced that *The Avengers* is next but they pushed it back once, which I thought was encouraging.'

Talking about being the film's executive producer, Favreau added, 'My involvement has yet to be determined on that project. You're not going to know about *Thor* for two years, what that really means. And *Captain America*, they haven't even started prepping yet. So there's a lot of discovery that has to take place before you can understand what *The Avengers* really is.'

Robert is now in a position he might never have thought he would be in – a complete saleable asset in the movie business. He is now in a position where his name attached to either a low-budget indie film or a popcorn blockbuster could go a long way to get a film green-lit. But this is a man whose feet start to itch when things seem to be just too good. Increasing maturity has put the brakes on that somewhat, but he says that, while acting keeps him 'on the go – but only momentarily', it does exhaust him a lot. Directing, he feels, would give him something new to offer.

As long ago as 2006 he confidently announced, 'I will direct a movie. It's a big pissing contest and I'll be a monster. I'll probably want to direct something I've written: I've got a killer science-fiction idea. I've got the story in my head, kind of like Mozart on ecstasy ... it's called *The New Math* and it's nuts, dude – so cool.'

No word on any of those projects yet but one script he is known to be interested in is a biopic of the 19th-century writer Edgar Allan Poe, best known for his tales of the macabre but also the inventor of detective fiction. Robert has hailed the script – written by Sylvester Stallone – as 'great'.

Even if none of these ideas comes to pass, the day of Robert's directorial debut is surely drawing nearer. In 2009 he confirmed to *Esquire*, 'I will not be able to remain happy and sedate being an increasingly hireable actor type. I think the best thing I can do for my soul and my own development would be to direct. It's really easy for me to do landgrabs with my day job and I still have a lot of passion for it but, if I had to guess, that would probably be my next move. I used to mention it every five years or so, between public humiliations. So it's been five years. It's time.'

Asked if he is having more fun now, Robert said, 'Absolutely more fun now, perhaps because I've lived more mistakes than I could possibly repeat. I'm kind of a professional troubleshooter in a sense. Having done so many films the less than optimal way, I tend to smell the end result of faulty process pretty acutely ... and hopefully help it be avoided by my co-workers.'

Even now, though, his friends still fear he will relapse, as Robert admitted. 'I can have the yoga teacher come to the door and if I don't answer it and he's waiting outside for me, he goes, "I thought you were fucking dead."

'How much support do I need?' he said to *Esquire*. 'Uh, tons?'

Robert has led a life so far of drama, troubles, fun, action and excitement. It's been never quiet, always eventful, but one thing has always remained constant for the actor – 'Go for broke and exempt all clichés if possible.'

Long may it continue.